Dating in a Digital World

The Woman's Guide to Online Dating

K. T. Harris

Table of Contents

Introduction

After my divorce, dating was a foreign concept to me. I had been married to the person I met in college. We were friends before we dated; we liked the same things, and spent most of our time together with our mutual friends—it had been effortless, really. Getting back into the dating game required effort, and I quickly learned that it required resilience, too! Everything changed so much because people now meet online through dating apps and social media. When I was ready to get back out there, I tried out online dating and it immediately scared me!

Hook-up culture took me completely by surprise as it became abundantly clear that sex was easier to find than meaningful connections. There also seemed to be an unsaid assumption that divorcees were there for a bit of fun and nothing else. What little interactions I had during this first attempt at online dating showed me there was a completely different language to learn. I didn't even know there were that many emojis on my phone! I quickly deleted the apps and decided that maybe I wasn't as ready as I thought I was. It was a whole new world, and I felt very old and out of touch with technology, even though deep down inside I knew I was neither.

With a little bit of research, and speaking to single friends and family members, I learned that I wasn't the only one. Even my twenty-something co-worker had had some horrible online dating stories! I asked her why she bothered with dating apps at her age and she asked me how else was she going to meet anyone. That seemed to be the general consensus; it's why I even decided to try it in the first place. Almost 30% of Americans use online dating apps and approximately 1 out of 10 adults you speak to nowadays are in a relationship with someone they met online (Vogels & McClain, 2023). While this may not seem like that many, if you consider your friend group, how many of them are using dating apps? Or how many stories have you heard, the good, bad, hilarious, and downright horrifying? Current statistics show that online dating experiences are 43% bad and 57% good (McClain & Gelles-Watnick, 2023). It's pretty close to a halfway split but it's nice to know that the good outweighs the bad!

All-in-all, whether you're a brand-new user or whether you are trying online dating again after a bad first experience, it is the easiest way to connect with new people. It can be incredibly overwhelming but the one thing I can tell you is that it will get easier with time. What I have learned over the years is that it does take a bit of a mindset change to embrace online dating and all that it is. Don't get me wrong, you don't have to change yourself in any way, or what you are looking for in a partner. However, you must go into online dating with clear intentions and understand how these apps work. It takes time to be able to navigate dating apps with confidence and be able to spot green flags among the red. This is why I wanted to write this book. I didn't have anything to guide me on my journey except a few supportive family members and friends. They may have been my cheerleaders to get back out there but very few of them actually knew what it was like "out there!"

Dating apps and social media have changed the dating landscape completely. While we all might find it overwhelming at first, it is convenient. Despite the outrageous stories or experiences that occur, you can make meaningful connections online. It can also be quite enjoyable with little risk involved if you know what to look out for. It took me a long time to try out different apps and find which one worked for me. It also took me time to learn how to set up a profile that truly reflected who I was and how to identify the profiles of people who aligned with what I was looking for. It's not about matching with anyone and everyone until you find "The One." You have the power to create your online dating experience to be what you want it to be. Many of us are too scared to admit that we want long-term, committed relationships because it seems that's the opposite of what others are looking for on dating apps. However, you don't have to hide what you want from online dating. In fact, being honest will help you find the relationship you desire.

This is what helped me find my spouse. We have been able to build a wonderful relationship together. We met through a dating app, navigated long-distance dating, and found that we were exactly what we were looking for, even though it did not seem like it at the time. I wanted to share what I have learned through my experience with you because it will save you time, some heartaches, and definitely a few headaches! It might even save you money because dating these days is not cheap! In this book, I will guide you through choosing the right dating app, creating a great profile, staying safe on dating apps, and communicating effectively (with words and emojis!). I'll also be discussing how to navigate break-ups and maintain relationships long-term.

It seems like a lot, but trust me when I say that it is possible. You just have to be willing to try and be open to learning the do's and don'ts of dating in the digital world. Even then, it will take time to find your unique path but once you do, you will be on your way to having great dating experiences and finding the relationship that you want. Shall we get started?

Chapter 1:

Navigating Online Dating

Online dating was popular ten years ago, but since 2017, the industry has seen exceptional growth. This was further multiplied during the COVID-19 pandemic when most people turned to dating apps to combat the loneliness of social distancing and the lockdown periods. Now, there are no less than 1,500 online dating sites and apps worldwide (Andre, 2021). I'm pretty sure most of us can name maybe 10 of them, but the number is representative of the variety available. This is understandable given that there are approximately 323.9 million dating app users around the world (Hadji-Vasilev, 2022). So, it's not only a matter of trying online dating, it's also about finding the right platform. In this chapter, we will journey through the advantages of online dating, picking the right platform, and creating a profile that truly showcases who you are and what you're looking for.

The Upsides of Finding Love Online

Traditional dating methods are timeless, but there is no denying that the digital age has changed the way people connect and find love. This transformation has not only expanded the pool of potential partners available to you, but it has also introduced a number of advantages that were once unimaginable. Let's take a closer look at these advantages while comparing them to traditional dating methods.

The Dating Pool

When it comes to traditional dating, we are limited to the people we are exposed to. Many times, it becomes a matter of our social circles, chance encounters, and introductions by others. However, if you really think about your daily routines, are you honestly looking for a relationship while getting lunch? As much as everyone would like to think that it is that simple, the fact is that we are often preoccupied with other thoughts. Personally, I am usually in such a hurry or thinking about what I need to do when I get back to work, that I barely notice the people around me. That is technically a bad habit, but it is also a consequence of the times we live in. In addition, even if we did see someone we were attracted to in the grocery store, how many of us would have the confidence to strike up a conversation?

Online dating has opened up a whole new avenue for us to explore. We are no longer limited to the people we encounter. The world has literally become smaller online as we can connect with people we would not usually have an opportunity to meet. People across the globe can match with each other on a dating app just as easily as they can match with someone from the next street. The online dating pool is significantly larger, thereby increasing your chances of finding meaningful connections. Furthermore, the fact that dating apps entail reviewing a person's profile, gives you a better idea of what you're getting into. All of us have been misled by good looks before, and having a bit more information makes all the difference!

Convenience

We live in busy times that hardly give us room to breathe, let alone date. Using a dating app allows us to move at our own pace and also meet people online from the comfort of our own homes. Traditional dating involves face-to-face meetings that involve aligning schedules and choosing a convenient place that satisfies both people. To make it sound rather profound but nonetheless true, online dating transcends temporal and spatial boundaries. It allows you to engage in meaningful conversations, share experiences, and build connections without the constraints of time and place which is one of the biggest drawcards.

Reduced Pressure

Traditional dating comes with awkward first encounters. Yes, I know that it's a part of the dating game but when first impressions make all the difference, those first encounters can misrepresent who we truly are. Consequently, many people lose out on potential second dates because the other person doesn't feel like there's instant chemistry. It becomes an "on to the next one" mentality. While online dating does not guarantee a great first date, it does give you time to get to know a person better so that you will be more at ease during a first date. There's a sense of anonymity, at least in the early stages of interaction, which enables people to share their thoughts, feelings, and interests more openly. As a result, online dating becomes a platform where individuals can build a foundation of connection before stepping into the real-world dynamics of traditional dating.

Compatibility Algorithms

One of the technological marvels driving the success of online dating is the implementation of sophisticated compatibility algorithms. The equivalent in traditional dating would be that one aunt or friend that everyone has who knows someone who would be "just perfect" for you. While the compatibility algorithms of online dating are not foolproof, they are undoubtedly better than family members who think they know you well. Most of the time we have an idea of what we want in a significant other, but it's not really concrete, or accurate for that matter. However, compatibility algorithms consider a multitude of factors, including interests, values, lifestyle choices, and relationship goals. By using data science, these platforms increase the likelihood of finding a suitable match.

Affordability

Dating these days is definitely not cheap. You have to consider the place, transport or fuel costs, food costs, the cost of movies—it doesn't matter that you're a woman, these costs all add up! Online dating avoids excessive costs by limiting the number of actual dates you go on. In addition, some people even opt for virtual dates first, before moving on to dates in person. This not only helps you get to know the person better but also ensures you feel comfortable and safe during this first meeting.

Affordability also comes into play when you consider the cost of a subscription to dating apps. Most apps offer a free version with limited functions that are quite satisfactory to many users. Subscription fees to most platforms are also quite reasonable and flexible in terms of the length of subscriptions and cancelations. It all depends on what you feel will work for you. Many people have been able to find spouses or significant others using the free versions of dating apps.

These are the main differences between traditional and online dating. They each have their own pros and cons, but online dating has provided us with more options that align with our busy schedules. Dating is never easy, but online dating makes it easier, especially for those of us who are entering (or re-entering) the dating world. It allows us to date at our own pace when we have the time, and be intentional about who we connect with. This increases the chances of finding a match while decreasing the nervousness and awkwardness associated with approaching someone in the real world.

Picking the Best Platform for You

When I finally sat down to download a dating app on my phone, I was overwhelmed by the sheer number of options. There were so many different platforms and I felt as if my entire future depended on this one decision. So, I sat down and went through the reviews and made my decision based on them. When I downloaded the app and set up my profile, I eagerly anticipated a flurry of activity that would lead me to my matches—and I was sorely disappointed with what I found. The few matches that came up were not at all what I was looking for. This led me to question my profile, the validity of the positive reviews I based my decision on, and even myself and my appeal to others. Extreme, I know, but dating tends to bring up all your insecurities even if it is online.

However, it took me some time to realize that you have to try out multiple dating apps to find the one that works for you. There's no perfect formula, no beginner's luck, and definitely no way of knowing that a platform is going to work for you. You have to ensure that it aligns with your dating goals, fits your budget, and suits your dating style. Not everyone likes to make decisions solely on a person's picture, while others may find it disconcerting if a person does not have a clear picture on their profile. There are so many little details that will either draw you to a platform or push you away. It is up to you to try out different platforms and decide which one fits your exact requirements because what worked for one person might not be the same for another.

There are six main factors that will help you choose a platform.

Your Goals

First and foremost, you have to identify your dating goals. This can be incredibly difficult and I have also noticed that some people feel ashamed to define their goals. However, no one else needs to know what you're looking for. Defining your goals will just help you identify the platform that will work best for you. There are some that target specific age groups, preferred relationship types, and even those specifically for the LGBTQ+ community. Thus, defining your goals will help narrow down the platforms to choose from and satisfy your requirements better.

Alignment

Once you have your goals, start looking at platforms that align with them. There will still be a fair number of platforms that will come up, but it will provide you with a list to begin with.

Check Availability

The first thing that will help narrow down your list is to check the availability of the platform in your region. While some platforms are global, others are only available in certain areas and might even exclude smaller towns or rural areas. Once again, this will still leave you with an extensive list, but it is the first factor that will help you trim it.

Evaluate the Matching Formula

Next up is the compatibility algorithms or matching formulas that platforms use. Depending on whether you're looking for a long or short-term relationship, platforms will have different ways to pair people. Some use complex algorithms that match you according to the information you provide in your profile, while others simply suggest people in your area. There are even some platforms that have complex questionnaires that will help them suggest compatible matches. You can use these criteria to narrow down your list further depending on what you are comfortable with.

Subscription Options

Most platforms will have free plans and subscription plans that unlock additional features. People have had success with both. I met my spouse through the free version of Tinder but I also know plenty of other people who were successful in finding partners with a paid plan. Your choice comes down to personal preference and budget, really.

Reviews

Lastly, reviews from online sources, friends, and family members can also help if you are still not certain. Ask questions about what you are unsure of, or why you are hesitant about certain platforms, and see what others have to say. It can help you determine if your concerns are valid or if you are hesitant because you are fearing the unknown.

These six factors will help you choose the best platform for you. Don't be confused or overwhelmed if you still have several options on your list. Online dating does not mean that you are jumping straight into marriage. Take your time, try them out, and get a feel for how they work. I tried one at first and ran away so quickly, I contemplated staying single for the rest of my life! However, by taking the time to step back, re-evaluate, do my research, and jump back in, I was able to find my spouse. That would never have happened if I didn't try again!

Some Popular Platforms

Some platforms are more well-known than others, purely because of their user base and success rates that are used in advertising. They are not the only platforms available, but they are the ones that most people turn to when they try dating apps and websites.

Tinder

Tinder is probably one of the most used dating apps in the world. In 2021 alone, they were the most installed dating app, having been downloaded by 67 million people (Dixon, 2023). It appeals to a broad demographic, including casual daters and those seeking more serious connections, and has a very simple interface. They were the first to pioneer the "swipe-right-to-like and swipe-left-to-pass" mechanism and it seems to have set the precedent for other dating apps that followed.

Tinder's ease of use is what grew its popularity alongside its location-based matching. It shows users potential matches in their vicinity, making it convenient to meet people in your area. However, this feature also made it infamous for being the "hook-up" app for fleeting encounters but many people have been able to find long-term relationships as well. There are both free and paid versions of the dating app and it remains one of the simplest platforms to use. However, since it is based on location, you are limited to who you are matched with, especially if you live in a small neighborhood.

eharmony

eharmony targets individuals looking for long-term, serious relationships, resulting in a user base inclined towards commitment. The compatibility algorithm used by this dating app is based on an 80-question questionnaire. It seems extensive but is actually quite popular given that approximately 15,000 people answer the questions daily (Calo, 2021). The answers to the questionnaire help guide the matching process, and although it does take some time, it is quite effective for people who are looking for potential long-term relationships. It is also available in 200 countries and matches are not limited by geography. Thus, the dating pool is massive.

eharmony also has free and paid options but you are only available to talk to your matches via the paid subscription. Given that this platform is for those looking for long-term relationships, a subscription is necessary to find potential matches but seems to be worth it as the app boasts of helping 2 million people find love!

Facebook Dating

Facebook has dominated the social media scene for years and many dating apps allow you to register using your Facebook account. However, Facebook now has its own dating app that allows users to link their profile effortlessly to the dating app. This seamless integration is appealing to people looking to venture into online dating with minimum effort. There are no fees involved and you may even be able to find out who has a crush on you within your own social circle.

When it comes to Facebook dating, you have to exercise caution. You have to verify that a Facebook profile is authentic and be aware of possible red flags like insufficient information, nicknames instead of real names, and no pictures. With this in mind, Facebook Dating can be extremely useful for an introduction to the online dating scene.

Match.com

Match.com is what you can consider as the "OG" of online dating, having emerged in the mid-90s. It has a diverse user base encompassing individuals of various ages and relationship preferences. Current estimates put the number of users at 39 million, with many of them being between the ages of 30 and 49 (Wong, 2022). Although the app allows users to state what type of relationship they are looking for, it does seem to be more suited toward those who are looking for serious relationships as opposed to hook-ups or casual dating.

Match.com allows you to create a detailed portfolio at your own pace. You don't have to answer all the questions, but the more you answer, the more compatible matches you can make. You also have the opportunity to review and reverse matches which are people with responses completely opposite to yours just in case you want to try the "opposites attract" approach. Like other apps, it has a paid version that unlocks extra features. However, the free version allows you to message one person a day which is still better than no messaging at all. Match.com does have a lot of potential but does not have as many users as other apps which does limit the people you will have contact with.

OkCupid

This dating app seems to be popular for people seeking relationships between the ages of 18 and 29 (Gilbert, 2021). It offers a variety of options and, in a first among dating apps, introduced multiple genders and orientations that cater to a diverse user base, including individuals seeking anything from casual dating to serious relationships.

The platform's compatibility algorithm is based on a mix of multiple-choice questions and user-generated responses, providing a balance between depth and simplicity. It can feel a bit time-consuming, but like with all dating apps, the more information you add to the profile, the better the algorithm can work to find your matches since OkCupid calculates match percentages based on user responses. The paid version of OkCupid doesn't exactly offer much more than the free but that does not mean that people don't subscribe. This is a popular app but it can definitely be a bit of a shock to the system for older users who aren't used to the new age dating lingo!

Bumble

Bumble's user base is characterized by a younger demographic (18-30). The platform is also known for empowering women by allowing them to make the first move. With over 50 million users, it is the second most popular dating app after Tinder (Utreja, 2023). Bumble also enables users to build extensive profiles and provides quirky prompts that they can complete. This helps users to evaluate profiles with a more laid-back approach.

The fact that women are in charge of whom they initiate contact with not only decreases the amount of unwanted messages one has to sift through but also reduces dating fatigue which is common with online dating. Another drawcard to Bumble is that the free option offers quite a bit of functionality. There are paid plans available but are not necessary for messaging potential matches. Furthermore, Bumble introduced BFF and Bizz which allows you to make new friends and professional connections if you're looking to expand your networks.

Hinge

With 23 million users worldwide, Hinge has a solid footing in the online dating world (Indah, 2023). It caters to users 24 to 35 years old who are looking to make genuine connections. Hinge has several aspects that are common in other dating apps. It uses a compatibility algorithm that encompasses both questions and prompts. However, rather than a casual swiping experience, Hinge employs an innovative liking system, where users can express interest in specific aspects of a potential match's profile, sparking more nuanced interactions.

The app also emphasizes user feedback through features like "We Met," encouraging individuals to provide insights on their matches and refining the app's algorithm for improved suggestions. There are limited features with the free version but it still offers functionality. It is almost a hybrid of Tinder and Bumble but focuses on helping users achieve long-term serious relationships.

HER

HER is a dating app that is specifically for women of the LGBTQ+ community. It provides a safe platform for women to match with others and has approximately 10 million users globally (Baluch, 2023). It has similar swipe options to Tinder, making it easy to use on your mobile device. HER has social communities that help women connect with like-minded individuals, chat, and share photos. The free version does limit users in how many messages they can send and how they search for matches on the app. However, the addition of the social communities is a large drawcard because that acts as a filter in itself. All in all, HER is a fast-growing dating app due to its particular niche and its ease of use.

These are just a few of the dating sites that you can try. They each have their user bases and subscription fees but you can make the best out of each of them by ensuring that you have clear dating goals and a profile that clearly reflects them.

Crafting a Profile That Stands Out

One of the things that can make or break your online dating experience is your profile. I know just how difficult it can be to find the balance between too little information and too much. There's also the slight worry at the back of your mind about whether it's safe or whether you should make yourself sound more interesting. The truth is, you will attract matches based on the information you provide. It is not merely a collection of photos and text, but a carefully curated representation of who you are, what you value, and what you seek in a partner. Crafting a standout profile is not just about attracting attention; it's about attracting the right attention.

Your online dating profile is the first impression potential matches will have of you. A well-crafted profile can make the difference between a passing glance and a meaningful connection. It serves as a glimpse into your personality, lifestyle, and aspirations. This is what you need to remember when putting it together. Let's take a closer look at each aspect of your profile and the steps you can take to ensure your goal is met.

Your Photos

1. The photos you put on your profile are really important. As much as the information we place in our profiles is also important, we live in a world where people will only read that info if they like what they see in photos. It is the reality of most dating apps, especially those with swipe functionality. Thus, you should choose your photos carefully by following these steps:

2. **Choose authentic photos**: Choose photos that authentically represent you in various aspects of your life. Candid shots and genuine smiles convey approachability and warmth.

3. **Showcase diversity**: Include a mix of photos that showcase different facets of your personality and interests. This diversity provides a more

comprehensive view of yourself for potential matches.

4. **Include solo and group shots**: While group photos can add social context, ensure there are clear solo shots so potential matches can easily identify you without confusion. Also, only include one or two, don't overdo the group shots because you want to keep the focus on you.

5. **Quality Matters**: Opt for high-quality, well-lit photos. Blurry or pixelated images can detract from the overall appeal of your profile.

6. **Avoid excessive filters**: While filters can be fun, don't rely on them too much. Some of them take away from natural features that make you unique. If you must use them, choose subtle filters that enhance your features and not change them completely.

To summarize the basics dos and don'ts:

Do: Smile genuinely, showcase your hobbies, and include recent photos that are of good quality.

Don't: Use outdated photos, rely solely on selfies, make a group shot your main profile pic, or include photos with ex-partners.

The Bio

The bio section is your opportunity to share more about yourself, offering depth and context beyond the visual cues of photos. Crafting a compelling bio involves striking a balance between showcasing your personality and maintaining an element of mystery. You want matches to want to know more about you and this is how you can do that:

1. **Start with a hook**: Begin your bio with a captivating hook that grabs attention. This can be a witty one-liner, an interesting fact, or a thought-provoking question. However, don't overthink it. Be yourself and make sure it's something you would say.

2. **Be genuine and positive**: Share your genuine interests and passions. Positivity is attractive, so focus on what you enjoy rather than what you dislike.

3. **Showcase personality**: Use anecdotes and specific examples to showcase your personality. If you're adventurous, share a brief story that highlights this trait. If you're a bookworm, use a quote from a book to describe yourself. Whatever it is, it should reflect and highlight your personality.

4. **Keep it short and sweet**: While it's essential to provide depth, keep your bio concise. Long paragraphs can be overwhelming, and a short bio maintains interest.

5. **Avoid clichés**: Steer clear of overused phrases or clichés. Instead of saying you love to travel, share a unique travel experience or destination.

Remember, your bio is what will seal the deal of whether a potential match contacts you. Avoid long sentences or providing too much detail because you want to add a bit of mystery that will keep them interested. However, don't leave everything hanging in the air as if you are a secret agent! It's a fine balance that takes some trial and error to get right, but it will be clear when you do.

Your Interests

When listing interests and hobbies, honesty is paramount. However, strategic presentation can enhance the attractiveness of your profile. The goal is to create a well-rounded image that resonates with potential matches while staying true to your authentic self. You don't want to be saying you like the outdoors, hiking, and extreme sports only to be terrified when your first date involves exactly that! Always remember that you want to get the right attention and base the information you provide on that. Here are the steps to follow when listing your interests and hobbies:

1. **Keep it real**: List interests that genuinely reflect your passions. This will help to foster connections with like-minded individuals.

2. **Balance common and unique interests**: Include common interests to appeal to a broader audience, but don't shy away from showcasing unique hobbies that make you stand out.

3. **Showcase depth**: Instead of listing superficial interests, provide context. If you enjoy reading,

mention your favorite genre or a recent book that left an impact.

4. **Mention activities**: Rather than listing generic hobbies, incorporate specific activities or experiences. For example, instead of saying you love music, mention your favorite concert or the last live performance you attended.

5. **Keep it simple**: While it's crucial to showcase diversity, avoid overwhelming your profile with an extensive list of interests. Focus on a few key passions that define you.

Once again, it's a fine balance of providing the right information without overloading your profile. Too much information is just as bad as too little. The best way to approach it is to consider your dating goals when crafting your profile. If you are seeking a serious relationship, emphasize values, long-term interests, and a commitment to growth. If you're open to more casual connections, highlight shared hobbies and interests that create a sense of companionship.

By maintaining authenticity, positivity, and a touch of mystery, your profile becomes a magnet for the right kind of attention, increasing the likelihood of meaningful connections that align with your dating goals. Remember, your online profile is not just a digital introduction but a crucial first step in the journey of online dating. You have to then learn how to communicate effectively with your matches, keeping them engaged and interested to know more about you. This is what we will be going through in the next chapter.

Chapter 2:

Effective Communication

The age of digital communication is interesting, to say the least. Many of us have difficulty judging tones, interpreting emojis, and trying to figure out if we should send something or not. We question replies, lack of replies, and open messages we wish we could unsee. Online dating greatly amplifies these feelings and increases anxiety because it feels like there is so much more at stake. You're trying to make a good impression while trying to remain authentic and interesting—it can be a lot for your brain to handle! In this chapter, we will go through the art of digital conversation, including what to say, what not to say, and how to use emojis and GIFs to your advantage. Just like learning a new language, it can be difficult, but it is definitely not impossible! Let's dive in.

Mastering the Craft of Real Talk Online

Chatting to someone online is very different from having a face-to-face conversation. You can't see their facial expressions, can't hear the tone of their voice, nor can you judge if they want to talk to you or not. It's as if we suddenly become aware of how influential knowing someone is to communicating. After all, when we text our friends and family members, there's very little misunderstanding because we know their tones and individual whims. When you talk to someone new online, you don't have that. However, what you do have is a bit of security.

You're talking to someone from behind a screen, meaning you will not be as nervous as you would be in person. This can sometimes embolden people, causing them to overshare or become a little too friendly too fast. Online communication is very much an art form. You have to initiate conversations that go beyond the surface but find the right pace so that it is an engaging online exchange. So, how exactly do you do this when social interactions are reduced to bite-sized comments and quick likes?

Well, for starters, meaningful conversations require honesty. Real talk allows individuals to share their thoughts, experiences, and emotions in a way that encourages listening, understanding, and interest. Both parties must be able to go back and forth, keeping the conversation flowing effortlessly. Superficial interactions or those that feel forced tend to fade away in the vast sea of digital noise. People quickly move on to find someone else who is easier to chat to. This is why you need to know how to initiate conversations and maintain the optimum pace to provide active engagement.

Tips for Initiating Conversations

You can't always wait for someone else to start a conversation. Dating apps like Bumble put women in charge of making the first move. It's not forward nor does it make anyone seem overly eager to the other person. In fact, they might even be grateful or relieved that you decided to reach out at all. With this in mind, here are some great tips to start meaningful conversations online.

Find Common Ground

The key to starting a conversation and steering it away from the boring pickup lines common in online dating lies in finding common ground. Whether it's a shared interest, a mutual acquaintance, or a recent event, identifying commonalities provides a solid foundation for more engaging dialogue. For example, if you notice that you both attended the same event, you could start by sharing your thoughts on the experience or asking them what they thought about it. Conversations that start this way, based on mutual topics of interest, are likely to be more enjoyable and more memorable.

Be Genuine and Vulnerable

Okay, this is a big one, and one that needs to be understood and embraced fully. Authenticity breeds connection. The more time you spend talking to someone, the more the conversation will expand to more than just the general topics of interest. Instead of sticking to safe topics, be willing to open up and share your thoughts and feelings. I know that this is a difficult step for most women as there is often this need to exude confidence in online dating. However, being vulnerable does not mean you are weak or insecure. In fact, it shows that you are confident and comfortable sharing with those you feel a connection with. Being vulnerable in your conversations allows others to reciprocate, fostering a sense of intimacy. Remember, it's okay to show your human side, complete with flaws and imperfections.

Ask Thoughtful Questions

Move beyond the typical "How are you?" and "What's your favorite color?" and ask questions that invite depth. Inquire about someone's passions, aspirations, or even their favorite childhood memories. Thoughtful questions demonstrate genuine interest and pave the way for more meaningful conversations. Think about the conversations you have in person and how you feel when someone asks you questions with genuine curiosity. It opens up the conversation completely, making it rewarding and enjoyable. Remember that you want to ask thoughtful questions that encourage conversation. It must not feel like an interrogation or one-sided!

Share Personal Stories

This connects with being genuine and vulnerable. In order to get to know someone, you must be willing to share personal stories. You can't expect anyone to form a connection with you without knowing you personally. I know that some of us are scared not only to share with others but also worry about the safety of sharing things with someone we have never met. This is a valid concern and you really shouldn't tell your entire life's story to everyone you match with on a dating app. However, when you connect with a potential match and the conversation naturally progresses it is okay to share snippets of personal stories that will help to connect further. You will know when this pivotal moment arises and should embrace the opportunity to take the conversation beyond small talk.

Know When to Speak and When to Listen

An important part of all communication is to practice active listening. Just as you must know how to initiate a conversation, you must also be aware of when to listen. No one should dominate a conversation. It should be a natural back-and-forth that entails learning about the other person just as much as you are telling them about yourself. This has to be in balance and you have to be present and listening to them instead of thinking about what you can say.

These tips can help you initiate a conversation and help to develop it into more than just small talk. Remember that as much as you can use common ground to initiate conversations, you must also be respectful of differences that everyone shares. In fact, discussing differences can help introduce you to diverse perspectives and help you identify preconceived notions that have influenced your life. It is only through open and honest communication that you can learn more about others and experience personal growth.

How to Pace Digital Conversations

We've all been there. It's not even an online dating problem because it happens in all chats. There will be a run of rapid texts and responses and suddenly it will fizzle out. Responses become slower because someone got busy or distracted or you keep missing each other's messages—it happens. However, when it comes to online dating, it leads you to question the entire situation. Did you bore them? Did they get tired of chatting with you? Maybe they found someone else more interesting. You can drive yourself crazy with the scenarios and leave you questioning the whole online dating process.

You must remember that online dating is a unique situation, but everyone on it also has their outside lives to attend to. You cannot expect constant communication just because we always have our phones with us. We all know that exciting feeling when you start dating someone and you look at your phone with every notification, hoping it's them. It's understandable, but at the same time, chatting to someone online cannot possibly be constant. The time you spend chatting must be meaningful and there must be a good pace that sustains the conversation and grows interest so that it can continue. Here's what you should aim to do to achieve this.

Pace Yourself With Responses

Finding the right balance in responsiveness is crucial. While it's important to reply in a timely manner to show interest, bombarding someone with a flurry of messages can be overwhelming. Gauge the other person's pace and mirror it to maintain a comfortable flow. Think about how you want to communicate as well. Many women feel overwhelmed with the number of responses they receive on dating sites and the type of messages they receive. Allow the chat to develop naturally and don't assume that more messages will signify more interest in your match. They might not see it the same way.

Embrace Intermittent Silence

In digital conversations, the fear of awkward silences can lead to hasty responses or meaningless texts to fill the void. Embrace the pauses as they give both parties a chance to reflect and contribute meaningfully to the conversation. A thoughtful response is often more valuable than a rapid one. In addition, as conversations progress, times, dates, and schedules should be discussed so that you can sync schedules and know that you have time to communicate.

If the silence drags on, and a potential match does not reply, don't feel bad about it. It happens more often than you think. People will ghost you when they have nothing more to say and want to keep looking for a match. They may not know how to communicate that and resort to silence. It's okay. You have lost nothing in these situations. Always remember that it is better to match with someone who knows how to communicate!

Respect Time Zones and Schedules

In our interconnected world, conversations on dating apps often span different time zones. Respect the other person's schedule, and be mindful of the times when they may be unavailable. Establishing a mutual understanding of each other's time constraints fosters a more considerate and sustainable communication flow. There is a mutual understanding that the pace will slow down at certain times. In this way, you are able to chat when you can and maximize this time "together."

Know When to Take It Offline

While online conversations are convenient, there comes a point when taking it offline can deepen the connection. Whether it's a video call, phone conversation, or an in-person meetup, transitioning to a different medium can provide a more immersive and authentic experience. However, this should not occur in every single match you make online. It is only when you feel comfortable to do so. Do not let anyone pressure you to do so otherwise. Pressure to do anything on online dating should be considered a red flag.

These tips should help you initiate a conversation and sustain it. Over time, as you develop a connection with someone, it will naturally progress to deeper conversations that allow you to learn more about each other. However, it won't always happen, and you need to know that that is perfectly normal. Not every match will lead to exciting and meaningful conversations but that is a natural part of dating in any form. You have to keep at it until you find the matches that matter.

Using Emojis and GIFs Wisely

There's no denying that emojis and GIFs have made communication easier. Even if people spoke different languages they could possibly have a conversation that contained nothing more but GIFs and emojis! However, what it means to you could mean something completely different to someone else in a different country. So, how do you effectively use this without it causing misunderstandings?

It's actually quite interesting because using emojis and GIFs has become more acceptable than words when it comes to first encounters online. In fact, research shows that initiating a conversation with a GIF is likely to increase responses by 30% and it is even shown to increase the chances of a conversation lasting longer (Alnuweiri, 2018). Thus, knowing how to use them properly could be the difference between getting a response and not. I understand that not everyone appreciates the use of emojis and GIFs over words, but we must also be willing to learn and understand the art of online communication. Many people think of them as effective icebreakers and to be fair, it probably hurts less when someone doesn't reply to a GIF than when they don't reply to a carefully thought-out opening message. Let's take a look at how you can use them in your online dating conversations.

Adding Tone and Emotion to Text-Based Conversations

One of the major advantages of using emojis and GIFs is that it allows you to add tone and emotion to text-based conversations. They're emotional punctuation marks, if you will, conveying the same signals as body language and facial expressions. Consider the difference between a plain "I'm excited to see you" and the same message accompanied by a cheerful emoji or an animated GIF of someone doing a happy dance. The latter not only conveys the excitement more vividly but also adds an element of playfulness and shared joy. In online dating, a well-timed wink or a playful GIF can communicate flirtation and interest in a way that words alone might struggle to achieve, and this is why it can be your greatest ally.

The Dos and Don'ts of Using Emojis and GIFs

Here's what you should do:

Consider Your Audience

Always consider the person you are chatting with when using emojis and GIFs. Judge the tone of the conversation and evaluate their use of them as well. This will give you a better idea of whether they would be receptive to them. In addition, when you see how they use emojis, you will have an understanding of what they mean to them and it won't get confusing.

Use Emojis to Enhance Conversations, Not Replace Them

Emojis and GIFs should complement your message, not substitute for it. You don't want the other person to feel as if they're translating hieroglyphics! Use them to enhance the emotional undertones of your words, but avoid relying on them as a crutch for effective communication.

Express Yourself Authentically

The use of emojis and GIFs should reflect your voice. Whether you're known for your dry humor or enthusiastic energy, let your chosen visuals reflect your personality. Do not use them to make yourself seem any different from who you are.

Use Them in Moderation

While emojis and GIFs can be powerful tools, resist the temptation to overuse them. A well-placed emoji or GIF is like a spice that enhances the flavor of a dish. If you add too much, it becomes overwhelming.

Use Them to Lighten the Mood

In certain conversations, a strategically placed emoji or GIF can help diffuse tension and lighten the mood. This can be particularly useful in defusing misunderstandings or navigating sensitive topics. However, this is always dependent on the person you are speaking to as some might not appreciate the attempt.

On the flip side, this is what you should not do:

Avoid Excessive Use

Flooding your messages with a barrage of emojis or GIFs can be overwhelming for the recipient. It may even seem like you don't know how to communicate effectively.

You should always maintain a balance and let your words carry the weight of your message.

Steer Clear of Misleading Emojis

Be mindful of the potential for misinterpretation. Similar to how some words in English mean something completely different in a different language, some emojis can carry different connotations depending on the platform or cultural context. Double-check that your chosen visuals align with your intended message.

In addition, try to avoid using the eggplant and peach emojis as they are often associated with sex and sexting on dating apps. Receiving these emojis early on in conversations should also be considered a red flag.

Avoid Use in Critical Communications

In critical or serious discussions, rely on the clarity of your words rather than the ambiguity of emojis or GIFs. These visual elements may trivialize the gravity of your message.

The use of emojis and GIFs can be useful in conveying a visual response or reaction to the messages you receive online. They inject humor into conversations, often breaking the ice and putting the other person at ease. However, you need to use them effectively and not rely on them to be interpreted as you see them. I always say that one should use them as much as they would like to receive them. In this way, you talk to people who match your communication style. The most important thing to remember is that they should enhance your words and not substitute them!

Tackling Online Harassment

Online dating has changed the way we connect and develop relationships. However, it also has an unfortunate and prevalent side effect: online harassment. In the pursuit of love and meaningful connections, users often find themselves facing unwanted advances, explicit messages, and, in some cases, outright harassment. Current statistics show that approximately 41% of adults in the United States have experienced online harassment of some form and this number increases to 70% if we consider the LGBTQ+ community alone (Vogels, 2021). It was also shown that 43% of men and 38% of women have experienced some form of harassment online and more women were subjected to sexual harassment than men (16% vs 5%).

Online harassment comes in many forms whether you are on a dating app or social media. Do not assume that the only form of harassment you will experience on a dating app or site will be sexual. Knowing the different forms of harassment will ensure that you have the upper hand and take the necessary precautions and actions should it happen to you.

Types of online harassment include:

- **Cyberstalking**: This type of harassment involves a person using the internet to harass you on different platforms. Receiving excessive comments or likes on posts on multiple social media sites can be an indication of cyberstalking, especially if you do not pass on info about your accounts or handles.

- **Online impersonation**: This is when someone uses your identity and information online without your consent.

- **Catfishing**: With this type of harassment, someone lies about their identity to trick you into a relationship online.

- **Doxxing**: This is when someone posts your personal information online with the intention of getting others to troll or harass you online or otherwise

- **Swatting**: Related to doxxing, swatting is when someone uses your personal information and makes a call to law enforcement with false accusations.

- **Trolling**: Most of us are familiar with trolling on social media. It is when someone makes unsolicited comments to make others doubt you or spread false rumors. This can also happen on online dating platforms if there are communities.

- **Sexual**: Sexual harassment occurs when someone sends or requests sexually explicit messages or images online. These are situations that are unwanted and unwelcome.

- **Revenge porn**: This type of harassment follows the distribution of sexually explicit images or videos without a person's consent. More often than not, it is done as revenge after a break-up, a form of manipulation, or a way to ruin someone's reputation.

I know this all sounds scary, but it is just what is possible online. You may not encounter any of them, but it is still worthwhile knowing what can happen. It is an unfortunate reality that we have to deal with in the digital age we live in.

Red Flags and Signs of Potential Harassment

To tackle online harassment effectively, it's crucial to be vigilant and proactive in identifying red flags and signs of potential harassment. While not an extensive list, the following are common indicators that should raise concern:

Unsolicited explicit content: If a conversation takes a sudden turn towards explicit or inappropriate content without your consent, it's a clear red flag.

Persistent and unwanted advances: Harassment often involves persistent and unwanted attention, where the other person disregards your boundaries and continues to pursue contact despite clear signals to stop.

Aggressive or threatening language: Any form of aggressive or threatening language is unacceptable. This includes derogatory comments, insults, or intimidation.

Stalking behaviors: If someone starts exhibiting stalker-like behavior, such as closely monitoring your online presence, tracking your location, or attempting to control aspects of your life, it's crucial to take action.

Manipulation: Beware of individuals who engage in manipulative behavior, such as gaslighting, guilt-tripping, or attempting to control your emotions.

These behaviors might start as a joke or they may be swept aside as one, but it is important that you pay attention. If something feels off or uncomfortable in a conversation, trust your instincts. Your well-being is the top priority, and it's okay to disengage from any interaction that makes you feel uneasy.

Steps to Take for Blocking and Reporting Harassers Online

It's important to note that if you do encounter any form of harassment online, there are steps you can and must take. This is to both protect yourself and others who could be experiencing the same thing.

Use the Blocking Features

Most dating apps offer blocking features that allow you to prevent specific users from contacting you. If you encounter harassment, use this feature promptly to cut off communication.

Report the Incident

Report the harassment to the platform. Dating apps usually have reporting mechanisms in place to address such issues. Provide details of the incident, including screenshots if possible, to support your case.

Check for Support Services

Some dating apps have dedicated support services to address harassment. Reach out to them, detailing your experience and seeking guidance on further steps.

Document Evidence

In extreme cases, it is necessary to keep a record of any harassing messages, images, or interactions. This documentation can serve as crucial evidence if you decide to involve authorities or take legal action.

Check and Adjust Privacy Settings

Review and adjust your privacy settings on the dating app. Limit the information visible on your profile to reduce the risk of unwanted attention.

Online harassment is not to be taken lightly. The impact it can have on an individual's mental health, sense of safety, and overall well-being is significant. Furthermore, if you do not report it, the person will continue to harass others on the platform. The digital landscape is convenient but also provides a space where harassers feel like there are no repercussions.

Speak to someone, whether it be a friend, therapist, or family member, if you are harassed. You may think because it's online, it doesn't make a difference, but it does. If you feel unsafe and feel the need to involve the authorities, it is within your rights to do so. Online harassment is very real and awareness needs to be built surrounding it. The more it gets spoken about, the more will be done about it. Dating apps have been great at updating their security measures, privacy options, and reporting features. If you do experience any form of harassment, speaking about it will help others and you will receive the support you need. There needs to be a culture of respect and accountability in the digital dating sphere, ensuring that everyone can pursue meaningful connections without fear of harassment or harm.

The factors discussed in this chapter will help you when communicating online. You should now have an understanding of what you should and shouldn't do when talking to potential matches online. However, it is a fine balance that takes time to get right and you should never beat yourself up if you have a less than ideal start when it comes to conversations. Just remember that finding someone you can speak to easily and transparently will make your online dating experiences enjoyable and possibly sustainable. In the next chapter, we will discuss how you can work toward taking these initial conversations and working toward building long-lasting connections.

Chapter 3:

Building a Connection

Statistics show that 1 in 5 relationships and a little more than 1 in 6 marriages begin online (Statistic Brain, 2018). That may not seem like a large number, but considering the amount of people who use online dating platforms, it is indeed significant. So, how do they turn that initial swipe into something long-term? Is there a secret to ensuring that you build a connection that turns into a serious relationship? This is what this chapter aims to answer. Let's start unlocking the secrets that will help you build the relationship you desire.

Why Shared Interests Matter

There are many factors that will influence the success of online relationships. However, common hobbies or passions can serve as a strong foundation for building deeper connections, fostering meaningful conversations, and sustaining relationships over time. While the saying "opposites attract" holds true in many cases, it's important to recognize that attraction doesn't always guarantee long-term compatibility. Initially, differences can create excitement and intrigue, but sustaining a relationship requires more than just the mystery of someone who is different from you.

Shared interests almost act as a stabilizing force, providing a common ground that bridges the gaps created by differences in personalities, values, or lifestyles. Thus, someone could be completely different from you personality-wise, but may like the same TV shows or have the same favorite restaurant as you. It is in these commonalities that you can bond with someone and build deeper connections. Having shared interests does not mean that you're dating or interested in someone who is a carbon copy of yourself. It just means that you will have a better chance of building a relationship. After all, couples who engage in activities they both enjoy are more likely to find fulfillment and satisfaction in their relationship. This is why it is always a good idea to be honest about your interests. It will be the bridge to connect you with others and potentially lead to a meaningful and satisfying relationship.

Examples of Shared Interests Leading to Meaningful Conversations and Activities

While not an extensive list, the following can give you some ideas of how to use your shared interests to develop more meaningful conversations and ultimately build relationships.

A Shared Love for Travel

Travel serves as a great example of a shared interest that can lead to meaningful conversations and activities. Two individuals who both have a passion for exploring new cultures and destinations can bond over their favorite travel experiences, bucket-list destinations, and travel aspirations. This shared interest not only sparks engaging conversations but can also lead to planning future trips together, providing a tangible and exciting aspect to the relationship.

Foodies Unite

The realm of food is another area where shared interests can be a powerful bonding factor. Individuals who share a love for cooking, trying new cuisines, or exploring local restaurants can engage in discussions about their favorite dishes, cooking techniques, and culinary adventures. Such shared enthusiasm can extend to cooking together, planning food-focused outings, and even experimenting with new recipes, creating shared experiences that strengthen the relationship.

Health and Fitness Goals

Health and fitness are increasingly popular shared interests in the realm of online dating. Individuals who prioritize an active lifestyle can connect over their favorite workouts, fitness goals, and wellness routines. Engaging in physical activities together, such as hiking, biking, or attending fitness classes, not only promotes a healthy lifestyle but also provides opportunities for shared experiences. This can be a great conversation starter and is a wonderful way for couples to stay fit and healthy together while strengthening their relationship.

A Passion for Literature

A shared love for literature can be a powerful bond between individuals. Whether it's a common appreciation for a specific genre, author, or book series, literature enthusiasts can engage in discussions about favorite books, memorable quotes, and the impact of literature on their lives. This shared interest can lead to activities such as book clubs, attending literary events, or even writing and exchanging stories, fostering intellectual and emotional connections.

Music Enthusiasts

Music is a universal language that transcends boundaries, making it a popular shared interest among individuals. Whether it's a shared love for a specific genre, band, or era, music enthusiasts can bond over concert experiences, favorite playlists, and the emotional impact of certain songs. This shared interest can lead to activities such as attending live performances, creating collaborative playlists, or even exploring each other's musical talents, fostering a vibrant and dynamic connection.

Other great examples of shared interests include creative arts, pets, and gaming. They all allow you to share what you are passionate about; and have enjoyable conversations in the process. It can be extremely rewarding to be able to talk to someone who shares the same interests as you because it forms a connection, there is an understanding between the two of you. Over time, you can use this connection to develop a meaningful, long-lasting relationship.

Mixing Screen Time With Face-to-Face Time

When you have settled into your online dating routines and you have matched with someone who you enjoy speaking to, how do you decide when to take it off-screen? Virtual interactions offer a level of convenience and accessibility that was previously unimaginable. You have the option of online chats and video calls that allow individuals to get to know each other without the nervousness that comes with physical proximity. This ease of communication is particularly beneficial for those with busy schedules, geographical challenges, or social anxieties, enabling them to explore connections at their own pace.

However, there is no denying that at some point, the relationship has to move into the real world. The essence of true chemistry and connection often lies in face-to-face interactions. You are able to see someone's facial expressions and body language when you speak to them and while first encounters can be nerve-wracking, they can also be amazing experiences. In addition, these face-to-face encounters often play a pivotal role in determining the depth and potential longevity of a romantic connection. The memories created during time spent together become the potential building blocks of a relationship.

These experiences are what most people are aiming for when they begin their online dating journey. However, how do you know when it is time to make the transition from screen time to face-to-face time off-screen? Let's find out!

Transitioning From Online Chats to In-Person Dates

Firstly, not every match made online leads to a meeting in real life, nor should you expect it to. You have to feel comfortable with meeting the person and while everyone has different timelines and expectations, you should not rush or be rushed into dates off-platform.

Here are some tips for making the transition and maintaining online communication.

Establish Mutual Interest

Before transitioning from virtual to physical interactions, it's crucial to ensure there is mutual interest and comfort between individuals. Engaging in meaningful conversations online, exploring shared interests, and finding common ground lays the foundation for a smoother transition to in-person meetings. This phase allows both parties to gauge compatibility and determine whether taking the relationship to the next level is a natural progression.

Choose the Right Time

Timing plays a significant role in transitioning from online chats to in-person dates. Rushing into a face-to-face meeting too soon may result in discomfort or awkwardness. On the flip side, delaying the transition for too long can lead to a lack of momentum or interest. Furthermore, some individuals really dislike digital communication and would prefer to meet in person, while there could be others who are more cautious and like to take things slow. You also have to consider your own comfort levels regarding this. Finding the right balance involves paying attention to the natural flow of the conversation and the level of connection established, ensuring that both individuals feel ready and excited about taking the next step.

However, you must also be cautious of situations where a match seems to be keeping things online. This is where open and honest communication will help you determine if the person is nervous, or if they are intentionally avoiding meeting you offline. The latter is a definite red flag as this could be someone who has no intention of meeting outside of the platform and is just enjoying the interaction online. Unfortunately, there are people who are in committed relationships or even married who use online dating platforms as an escape or to live out some sort of fantasy life. They keep all communication online and avoid meeting or chatting off-platform. Don't make the mistake of thinking all matches who don't want to meet are shady, but trust your instincts if communication efforts lead to that conclusion.

Select a Comfortable Venue

Choosing the right venue for the first in-person meeting is essential in creating a comfortable and enjoyable experience. Opting for a neutral and relaxed setting, such as a coffee shop, park, or casual restaurant, provides a conducive environment for open conversation and connection. Avoiding overly intimate or formal settings initially allows for a more organic and relaxed interaction, setting the stage for a positive experience.

Maintain Virtual Momentum

Even as the relationship progresses to in-person interactions, it's important to maintain a level of virtual communication. Online chats, video calls, and other digital interactions continue to play a role in sustaining connection and intimacy, especially in situations where physical proximity remains a challenge. Regular communication through these channels allows for ongoing sharing of thoughts, experiences, and emotions.

Incorporate Shared Online Activities

In addition to traditional online chats, incorporating shared online activities can further enrich the relationship. The COVID-19 lockdown period introduced us to all sorts of online activities to stay connected. Whether it's playing online games, watching movies together through streaming platforms, or participating in virtual events, these shared activities provide a bridge between the digital and physical worlds. They allow individuals to connect in creative ways, fostering a sense of togetherness even when physically apart.

The key to a successful and well-rounded relationship lies in recognizing the strengths of both the virtual and physical realms. Virtual interactions offer a platform for initial connection, while face-to-face meetings provide the depth, intimacy, and shared experiences that form the foundation of a lasting connection. Each realm complements the other, contributing to the holistic growth and development of the relationship.

Balancing screen time and face time may come with its challenges, such as scheduling conflicts, geographical differences, and sometimes even reluctance to strike a balance; but it is something that must be done. Navigating these challenges, together with open and honest communication, is the path to a solid and stable relationship. Understanding preferences, comfort levels, and expectations ensures that both individuals are on the same page and can move forward together.

Be Prepared to Encounter Some Ghosts

Whether you're dating or not, you've probably encountered a ghost. You know, those people who chat with you and make you feel as if there's a connection, and then, poof! They disappear without a trace. The term "ghosting" reflects the abrupt and unexplained nature of the disappearance, as if the person has become a "ghost" in the relationship. You're left wondering if you have said or done something wrong, and you will probably never find out. Ghosting has become quite the norm in our society—the digital age has made it even easier. It really is poor communication etiquette and it can take quite an emotional toll on people.

A recent poll of 5,000 Americans showed that almost 60% of people say they have been ghosted when it comes to dating and approximately 45% have ghosted someone else (Prendergast, 2023). These stats are regardless of gender or circumstance and purely based on their responses regarding ghosting. The same poll revealed that 67% of people admitted to ghosting people that they have chatted to on a dating app but never met in person. This proves the earlier point of how the digital age has made ghosting easier. There seems to be a notion that because you're just chatting to someone, you don't have to respond to them when you decide that there's no spark or if you meet someone more interesting. However, what everyone fails to realize is that this behavior has a negative impact on the ghost and the person they're ghosting.

The Impact of Being Ghosted

When you have been ghosted by someone, it can have a ripple effect not only on your dating life but also on your emotional and mental well-being. Many people fail to recognize that they are actually hurting someone just because they don't know them personally or well enough. Let's take a closer look at what happens when someone is ghosted.

Feelings of Rejection and Inadequacy

One of the largest and most immediate impacts of being ghosted is the overwhelming sense of rejection. The sudden disappearance of communication leaves one questioning their worth, attractiveness, and overall adequacy. Imagine feeling like you are really connecting with someone, and then they disappear without a word. You don't know what happened which would leave you questioning everything, including yourself. There's no closure, no known cause, and no way of finding out. This can create a deep emotional wound that can linger long after the event.

The Development of Trust Issues

Another consequence of being ghosted is that it can negatively influence your overall trust in the online dating experience. It can even spill over into all your relationships, resulting in an emotional guardedness that prevents you from connecting with others. In an attempt to protect yourself from being ghosted, you take a step backward by being hesitant to let yourself be vulnerable to anyone. This will impact your dating life and potentially prevent you from developing future relationships.

The Negative Impact On Self-Esteem

The sudden silence that comes with ghosting can significantly impact self-esteem and self-image. It automatically becomes a matter of "it must have been me," because why else would someone just stop communicating? Unfortunately, this type of thinking will have a negative impact on one's self-esteem that will carry over into other dating experiences. You will be left always doubting or second-guessing yourself which then leads to feelings of insecurity that extend further than online dating and spill over into social and even professional settings.

The Impact of Being a Ghost

Ghosts are scary, right? No one really wants to encounter a ghost, and it's no different in the dating scene. Ghosts give themselves a bad reputation, but more so than that, being a ghost also negatively impacts you as a person. Most people think that ghosting someone won't have any repercussions, but it truly does. Here's how:

The Problem With Avoidance

When you ghost someone, there may be some temporary relief in the silence because it allows them to avoid uncomfortable or confrontational conversations. However, this avoidance, while providing a short-term solution, can lead to long-term consequences. You might find that over time, you may experience a sense of guilt and moral discomfort. Even if you don't, there is also the aspect of not being able to communicate effectively. While ghosting may seem like the only choice, it really is just a way to avoid an uncomfortable conversation.

Limits Personal Growth

Ghosting can have implications for the emotional intelligence of the person behind the act. When we talk about emotional intelligence, we mean the ability to recognize and understand one's own emotions as well as those of others. Choosing to ghost someone may reflect a lack of emotional maturity or an unwillingness to engage in difficult conversations, hindering personal growth. If you are unable to identify the situations that require communication, you are not in a good place to pursue relationships that require this on an almost daily basis.

Feelings of Regret

Over time, the person who initiates ghosting may experience feelings of regret. As they navigate future relationships, the realization of the impact of their actions on the other person may lead to a deeper understanding of the importance of open communication and empathy. This may even occur after they have been ghosted themselves. This self-awareness can contribute to personal growth and the development of healthier relationship practices in the future—but only if you learn from the experience.

Understanding the dual impact of ghosting can give you perspective and help you understand why it occurs. Having this understanding is also an important part of personal growth. You can stop it from impacting you negatively if you have been ghosted and ghosts can learn to step away from ghosting behaviors and try alternative options—which is what we will go through next.

You Don't Have to Be a Ghost

You don't have to resort to ghosting if you're ready to move on. There are simple steps to take that can save both you and the other person from any harm.

Open Communication

One alternative to ghosting is open communication. Instead of abruptly ending communication, individuals can choose to express their feelings honestly and clearly. Whether it's a lack of romantic interest, personal circumstances, or a desire to pursue other connections, communicating these reasons allows for closure and understanding. This approach, while potentially difficult, fosters a culture of respect and transparency in online dating.

Expressing Intentions Early On

Expressing intentions and potential concerns upfront establishes a foundation of transparency and mutual understanding. This proactive approach encourages a healthier dating environment where both parties can make informed decisions about the trajectory of the relationship. This doesn't have to be an upfront list of expectations for the relationship that will overwhelm you. Instead, aim to be open about what you are looking for in a relationship and come to a mutual understanding of what to do if either party doesn't feel as if the connection is working out.

Provide Constructive Feedback

This one can be a little tricky. However, the right approach allows you to leave without ghosting someone. When the decision to end communication is based on specific issues or concerns, you can be honest and communicate this to the other person. It can be valuable feedback that allows others to learn and grow from the experience, improving their future interactions and relationships. It does require quite a bit of tact and empathy, but if done right, it can be a far more rewarding conversation for both people.

When it comes to dating, it is crucial that we recognize that people have different preferences, expectations, and boundaries. We need to be able to communicate effectively and exhibit empathy and understanding. In addition, being clear in your dating goals will prevent you from leading people on when you know the match is not going to work out. It's quite typical that we may not know what we want in a partner, but we are generally clear about what we don't want and this is what should be a part of the conversation so that matches can continue with a lesser chance of ghosting. The importance of maturity and respect cannot be overstated in the realm of online dating. While it may be tempting to take the easy way out through ghosting, recognizing the human aspect of these interactions is crucial for everyone's well-being.

Navigating the Murky Waters of a Situationship

Another aspect of modern dating is the concept of the "situationship." Defined as being a relationship dynamic that lacks the clarity and commitment of a traditional romantic partnership; a situationship can be fun at the beginning, but very rarely stays that way. It often lacks defined boundaries, labels, or clear expectations. In a situationship, individuals may engage in romantic or intimate activities without a mutual agreement or understanding of the nature and future of the relationship. There is no need to define the relationship when you're still figuring it out. However, when this gets to a point where one person is ready to take it to next level, and the other is not, the situationship can prevail and leave one person feeling unhappy and dissatisfied.

How to Identify if You're Stuck in a Situationship

There are clear signs of a situationship and being aware of them will allow you to decide if it's time to talk about a relationship or time to move on. Here are the signs you need to look out for:

Undefined Boundaries

In a situationship, there is a lack of clearly defined boundaries, making it challenging for individuals to understand the nature and limitations of the relationship. There are no rules about when is date night or if you can see other people. There are no boundaries that would make the situationship a relationship. Even the labels like "boyfriend" or "girlfriend," are lacking, leaving both parties in a gray area. Thus, if you find the person you're seeing is reluctant to define the relationship or even put a label on it, you're in a situationship.

Lack of Open Communication

One of the primary signs of a situationship is a lack of open and honest communication about the nature of the relationship. If discussions about commitment, exclusivity, or future plans are consistently avoided or dismissed, it may indicate that you are in a situationship.

Inconsistency

In a committed relationship, there is typically a mutual investment of time and effort to nurture and grow the connection. In a situationship, however, these investments may be inconsistent or sporadic, reflecting a lack of commitment and priority. There's also a sense of instability since all factors regarding commitment, and even monogamy, are unknown.

Lack of Planning for the Future

A clear distinction between a relationship and a situationship lies in the consideration of the future. If discussions about future plans, shared goals, or long-term commitments are consistently avoided, it suggests that the relationship lacks the commitment associated with more traditional partnerships.

These are the four red flags of situationship. If you have identified with flags at any point, you need to decide how to move the relationship forward or move on.

Moving Forward or Letting Go

I know that navigating a situationship can be tough, but you need clarity in order to have the relationship that you desire. This is especially true if you started off with clear intentions but deviated from them because you found a match who could be a potential partner but decided to give it some time. It's perfectly fine to be patient if that is what you want. However, if the situationship has gone on for too long, you need to re-evaluate. Let's go through some steps that can help you with this.

Time to Self-Reflect

The first step in navigating a situationship is engaging in self-reflection and conducting an honest assessment of your own desires and expectations. Clarify what you are seeking in a relationship, whether it be commitment, exclusivity, or a shared future. Understanding your own needs is crucial in determining whether the situationship aligns with your relationship goals.

Start Talking

For those seeking clarity in a situationship, initiating open and honest communication is vital. Addressing the ambiguity, expressing your feelings, and discussing expectations for the future can help bring clarity and transparency to the relationship. While this conversation may be challenging, it is an essential step toward gaining mutual understanding.

Even discussing mutual goals and aspirations can provide insight into whether both individuals are on the same page regarding the future of the relationship. If there is a misalignment in long-term goals or a lack of shared vision, it may be an indication that the situationship is not serving anyone's needs.

Set Boundaries

You need clear boundaries to start transitioning a situationship to a relationship. Clearly communicate your own boundaries and expectations, and encourage your partner to do the same. Setting boundaries helps define the parameters of the relationship and provides a framework for moving forward or deciding to part ways. You both will know whether you are willing to maintain these boundaries or not.

Ultimately, decisions regarding the future of the situationship should be rooted in self-respect. If the relationship aligns with your goals and provides the emotional security you seek, consider moving forward. However, if the situationship is causing emotional distress, compromising your well-being, or hindering your personal growth, it may be time to consider ending the relationship. I know this is easier said than done, but relationships require maturity, communication, and understanding. If you are unable to do this, then it is not the time to be moving into a relationship.

Recognizing the signs of a situationship, initiating conversations about expectations, and setting clear boundaries are essential steps in gaining a deeper understanding of the relationship. Whether the decision is to move the relationship forward or to end it, the emphasis should be on a commitment to personal and collective growth as a couple. This is what dating entails nowadays and if things don't progress as you expect, all you can do is learn from the situation and move on to the next one with clearer objectives and knowledge of what to avoid. This chapter has given you the vital information you need to navigate building a connection with a match online and the red flags to look out for. In the next chapter, we will discuss the necessary steps to take to ensure your safety when pursuing relationships online and when they move off-screen.

Chapter 4:

Staying Safe

Online dating has to move into the real world at some point. It's the natural progression of the entire process and an exciting time to get to know people better. However, this is also a time to exert caution. You may have been talking to someone online for a while, but as a woman, you have to be cautious when setting up first dates with anyone. Approximately 36% of women who use dating apps in the U.S. believe that these platforms are not all that safe (Anderson & Vogels, 2020). This is due to not only the harassment they face online but also the experiences they have when meeting a person for the first time.

This is not meant to scare you away from using an online dating platform. Instead, it is just a way to educate you on the importance of safeguarding yourself and your information while using dating platforms. There are certain red flags to look out for, and steps you can take to remain safe both on and off-screen. This is what we will be going through in detail in this chapter so that you can find a match online while still staying safe.

Why Safety Can't Be Ignored

Firstly, I want to highlight some common scenarios that women have found themselves in while dating online. This is not to scare you but to demonstrate why safety can't be ignored when using dating platforms. Being aware of what can happen will help you put steps in place to minimize the chances of it happening to you.

Fake Profiles

There are a lot of fake profiles lurking on online dating platforms. It's not easy to spot because some people have fake information in between some true elements, while others are completely fake with stock photos and a completely false persona to match. The intentions behind these profiles can also range. There have been women who have experienced catfishing, stalking, and even identity theft from interacting with these fake profiles.

Dating Someone Who Is Already Attached

Sometimes connected to fake profiles, some people already have a partner or spouse and still have dating profiles. As mentioned earlier, they could be pursuing women online as a form of escapism or living a fantasy life with no intention of moving things forward. Some women have even gotten into serious relationships off-platform, only to find out later on that the person was or is in another relationship. It's quite an ordeal to discover that you may have been the reason a marriage or relationship ended. However, you were lied to by the guilty party as well.

Beware the Long Con

Many women have been conned out of money on online dating platforms and social media. In fact, recent statistics show that online scams have resulted in a whopping $547 million being lost by people to an online romantic interest in 2021 alone (Stouffer, 2023). When it comes to these encounters, these people are not afraid of the long con. One unlucky teen even registered at a university to be with her long-distance boyfriend in another country only to find out that the university and the boyfriend did not exist (Mukherjee, 2019).

These con artists always have clever excuses for why they can't meet, or why they need money. Some even keep asking for small amounts over a long period of time. The women who get scammed are left feeling gullible, naive, and without a significant amount of money.

Dating Someone With Ulterior Motives

Getting to know the people you match with online is exciting. It can all feel like it's going smoothly or that you have met the perfect person. However, some women have had the unfortunate experience of being in a relationship with a person who was using them for something else. Some meet people from different countries who pretend to be the ideal partner but in reality, they're just looking for an opportunity to move abroad. Others have the unfortunate experience of really falling hard for someone just to find out they were just using them to make someone else jealous. There are even those individuals who are just looking to get over a broken heart by finding someone to rebound with. In all these instances, the person has very different reasons for pursuing a relationship with you than making a meaningful connection.

Stalkers

Encountering stalkers on a dating platform can be scary. Some women have reported that people make multiple accounts and send them inappropriate messages and pictures. Stalkers are also known to learn as much as possible about a person and start pursuing them outside the dating platform. This can be on social media, at their workplace, and even frequenting places that they share pictures of. What's even more difficult is that stalkers can set up fake profiles, keeping their real identities hidden.

Photos Being Used Inappropriately

Another scary situation that women find themselves in online is when their photos are used inappropriately and without their consent. We have all heard of the infamous "send nudes" message, but even normal profile pictures have been used with ill intent. One woman even reported getting photos and videos of a man masturbating to her profile pictures (Mukherjee, 2019). She was so traumatized by the incident that she now doesn't post her picture on dating sites at all, which negatively impacts the matches she makes.

Other women have had their photos stolen and used to create fake profiles on different dating sites than the one they're on. These fake profiles are then used to catfish or scam other unsuspecting users.

These are just a few instances of why safety can't be ignored when using online dating platforms. As much as the site or app may have security measures in place, there will always be those who are able to slip through the cracks or come up with ways to avoid detection. It is important that you are careful with what information you share and be observant of the information that others share with you. We live in an age where we have to know how to ensure our safety in every situation.

Deciding What Personal Information to Share

Whenever we mention setting up your online dating profile, we always talk about balance. The more information you share about hobbies, interests, and yourself in general, the better matches you can make. However, you should always prioritize your safety and this can leave you confused about what information to share. On one hand, sharing too much personal information can expose individuals to identity theft, cyberstalking, and other online threats. On the other, not sharing enough information could cause people to question your authenticity. Therefore, having an understanding of what information is generally safe to share and what should remain private is crucial for a secure and positive online dating experience.

General Guidelines for Safe Information Sharing

Here are some general tips regarding information sharing.

You Can Use a Pseudonym

Some people opt to use a pseudonym or username instead of sharing their full name. It is somewhat of a controversial option as some people think of it as deceptive. However, you're not lying about who you are. It allows you to maintain a degree of privacy while still presenting an authentic version of yourself.

Avoid Disclosing Your Address

Instead of providing your specific address, consider using more general location information. Mention your city or neighborhood, but avoid sharing details that could pinpoint your exact whereabouts. This precaution protects your safety and adds a layer of anonymity.

Choose Photos Wisely

Photos are a central component of online dating profiles, but it's important to be selective about what you share. We often focus on how we look in the photo and forget to check what's in the background. Avoid posting photos that reveal sensitive information, such as your home address, your place of work, or your license plate.

Avoid Workplace Information

While mentioning your profession is common on dating profiles, be cautious about divulging specific workplace details. You should always avoid disclosing the name of your company or providing information that could make it easy for someone to track down your workplace.

Contact information

Most online dating platforms have built-in messaging systems, eliminating the need to share personal contact information immediately. Refrain from sharing your phone number or email address too early in the interaction to avoid potential misuse of your contact details.

Financial Details

In no way are your financial details necessary to share. It doesn't matter if you're a financial analyst and a match jokingly asks you about investments, you don't need to disclose anything regarding your financial situation, salary, or investments. This is something that has no place during online dating conversations and should not be entertained while chatting.

So, what can you share? Here's a simplified list:

- your hobbies and interests

- educational background

- general location

- your profession/job title

Spotting Warning Signs in Online Profiles

A well-crafted online profile serves as a virtual introduction, but it's essential to navigate with caution and awareness. It's essential to be aware of warning signs that may indicate deceptive or unsafe intentions. We have gone through a few already, but here are some that relate directly to online profiles.

Vague Information

One of the most significant red flags in an online dating profile is the presence of vague or limited information. Profiles that lack specific details about a person's interests, values, or background may indicate a lack of authenticity or a reluctance to share genuine information. A lack of transparency in the early stages of online interaction can be a cause for concern.

One Photo

Profiles featuring only one photo often raise suspicion, as a single image may not provide a comprehensive representation of the individual. A reluctance to share multiple photos could be an attempt to conceal certain aspects of the person's appearance or lifestyle. In general, diverse and genuine photos contribute to a more transparent and trustworthy profile. However, evaluate photos critically because we all know how convincing edits can be!

Offensive or Aggressive Language

The language used in an online dating profile can reveal a lot about someone's attitude and approach to relationships. Profiles containing aggressive, offensive, or disrespectful language may signal potential issues in communication and compatibility. Language is a powerful tool for expressing values and intentions, and red flags can emerge when it is used inappropriately.

Unrealistic Details

Inconsistencies in the information provided in an online profile can be indicative of deceptive intentions. You must be wary of profiles that present conflicting details about personal characteristics, interests, or life circumstances. Unrealistic or overly embellished information may also suggest a lack of authenticity. You may also find that the conversations you have with certain people will not match the information they have on their profile. It's wise not to get caught up in the excitement and pay attention if these details match.

Not Respecting Boundaries

Some people will push you to move communication off-platform or try to encourage an in-person meeting despite you having clear boundaries regarding this. They might even send sexually explicit messages even though you have set the record straight about what you are looking for in a relationship. Not being able to respect these boundaries is a clear red flag and you must not be forced to do something you are not comfortable with, even if it means losing a match.

Avoidance

Someone willing to engage in open communication is a significant part of making successful matches online move further along. Red flags may appear when individuals actively avoid discussions about their background, intentions, or expectations. Profiles that resist open communication or ask you for more details but are reluctant to provide them about themselves are definitely people you should be wary of.

You need to trust your instincts when it comes to red flags. Trusting your instincts involves paying attention to gut feelings and emotional responses when engaging with online profiles. If something feels off or raises concerns, it's crucial to acknowledge these feelings and not push them aside. You don't have to avoid the person or ignore them completely, but simply be alert when speaking to them. These are just the necessary precautions to take to ensure your safety before pursuing a relationship any further.

How to Meet Safely Face-to-Face

Meeting someone you connected with online is the natural next step of the dating process, giving you the potential to build a relationship in the real world. However, the excitement of this transition should be coupled with a commitment to safety and mindfulness. There always needs to be balance when it comes to online dating and in this case, it's crucial to keep a clear head. You can't afford to get sloppy about safety at this stage when you have been careful online!

A Step-by-Step Guide to Meeting

We've put together a step-by-step guide to help you stay safe when meeting anyone off-platform.

1. Choose Public Spaces

When planning the first face-to-face meeting, selecting a public place is the first step to staying safe. You should always opt for well-trafficked locations such as cafes, restaurants, or parks, where there is a constant flow of people. Public spaces will provide a level of security and create a comfortable environment for initial interactions.

2. Choose to Meet During the Day

This one is a little hard depending on your schedule. However, choosing to meet during the day is generally considered safer for first encounters. The visibility and familiarity of daytime surroundings contribute to a more secure environment. You are able to speak freely with someone while still being able to observe your surroundings. Additionally, scheduling a daytime meeting allows for a casual and less pressured interaction. Many people find it less intimidating than heading to a romantic restaurant or a crowded bar.

3. Tell a Friend

Before the meeting, inform a trusted friend or family member about the details. I know that some people like to keep the fact that they're dating online on the down low, but you have to tell someone at some point. However, if you really don't want to, just tell them you have a date without telling them how you met. Share the relevant information with them, including the location, time, and the person's name. You can also establish a communication plan, such as checking in before and after the meeting with a simple text message. It might seem excessive but is necessary in the times we live in.

4.   Find Your Own Way

To maintain control over your departure, it's always a good idea to use your own transportation when meeting someone for the first time. Whether driving yourself to the date or using a rideshare service, having your own transportation allows you to leave the meeting at your discretion, providing an additional layer of safety.

5.   Don't Drink too Much

If the first meeting involves a venue where alcohol is served, it's essential to exercise moderation. Limiting alcohol consumption allows for clear-headed decision-making and enhances overall situational awareness. However, even more important, is that staying sober on a first date allows you to have meaningful conversations and remember your first meeting fondly. No matter how nervous you are, overdoing the alcohol will completely skew the meeting and might even give the other person the wrong impression of you. Staying alert and focused contributes to a safer and more enjoyable experience.

6.   Keep Your Personal Items Secured

This may seem like an overly cautious one, but it is definitely better to be than regret it later on. Keep your belongings, such as your purse, phone, and wallet, close to you to prevent the risk of theft during the meeting. You might think that it's a lot of effort for someone to steal from you, but you can never know what may happen. There was a woman who had her entire bag stolen by a guy she met on Tinder. They had chatted for weeks and she felt comfortable enough to meet him for lunch. After several hours together, she got up to use the bathroom and left her bag at the table with her date. When she returned, he was gone and so was her bag (Staudinger, 2017). Therefore, you rather be cautious than become the next unfortunate victim.

7. Keep Your Wits About You

Maintaining awareness of your surroundings is crucial for physical safety. Be mindful of things like exits, emergency exits, and the general layout of the venue. It's also a good idea to pay attention to your date's body language and have a general idea of the area you are meeting in if you are not familiar with it. Staying aware allows you to navigate the space confidently and respond effectively to any unexpected situations so you won't be caught off-guard.

8. Manage Your Expectations

Not related to physical safety, but more toward safeguarding your mental and emotional health, you have to approach first meetings with realistic expectations. While online interactions provide valuable insights, meeting in person may bring additional aspects to light. The person may be charming when they speak to you, but they could be horrible to waiters or other service providers you encounter on your date. Likewise, they could be a big talker online but may feel shy or intimidated when they see you in person. Always aim to be open-minded and allow the interaction to unfold naturally, without imposing rigid expectations both on yourself and the person you are meeting.

9. Communicate Clearly

Effective communication is crucial at all stages of the dating process. However, during first encounters in person, it becomes even more important. This is the time that you can express your thoughts, feelings, and intentions while also actively listening to your potential partner. Being together, face-to-face can enhance the experience and allow you to deeply connect with one another. It is also the time to ensure that boundaries are respected and both parties know what to expect moving forward. This makes communication an integral part of maintaining physical, emotional, and mental safety.

10. Have an Exit Plan

Lastly, we joke about this all the time, but having an exit plan is crucial. We all hope for an enjoyable and meaningful interaction but if things take a turn for the worse, you need to make a smooth exit. Having a friend or family member know about the exit plan and how to execute it is the best way to quickly leave if things become uncomfortable.

This is your guide to staying safe when meeting potential partners face-to-face. As online dating continues to be a prevalent means of meeting potential partners, fostering a culture of safety is essential. Don't be afraid to ask questions and speak to others if you have any hesitations. It's not being paranoid, but being a responsible adult who is aware of potential dangers. Remember to always trust your instincts and know that you can leave at any point if you are uncomfortable. Your safety should always be your priority.

Navigating Consent and Boundaries Online

Traditional dating makes it easy for boundaries to be known. Your words, actions, and body language can clarify any confusion and it's easy to see when you are uncomfortable in a situation. Most of the time, this is enough for others to respect your boundaries. In contrast, the digital world blurs the lines of personal space and consent. There are times when you will feel uncomfortable and as if your boundaries are not being respected. This makes it crucial to communicate them effectively and be mindful of the boundaries of others.

Tips for Communicating Boundaries Clearly Online

It can be difficult to communicate your boundaries or talk about the importance of consent without ruffling a few feathers. This is because many people don't really think about boundaries online and may find the whole conversation unnecessary. I'm not quite sure whether it's because of the physical distance or the anonymity that comes with an online profile, but there are those who just don't understand the need for it. However, dating requires boundaries and an understanding between people no matter how it occurs. Always remember this and the fact that meeting people who understand consent and the need for boundaries are the kind of people you want to date in the first place!

Here are some great tips for making boundaries clear online:

1.   Identify Them

Before entering the world of online dating, take time for self-reflection to identify your own boundaries and comfort levels. You can't communicate your boundaries if you are not sure what they are yourself. Understanding your needs and limits is crucial for effective communication and will be the key to moving forward.

2.   Make Your Communication Options Clear

Choose communication channels that align with your comfort level. Whether it's messaging on the dating app, emails, or video calls, establishing clear communication channels will help maintain transparency and ensure there is no confusion. In addition, have boundaries regarding pictures. Let people know if you are uncomfortable with sending or receiving pictures. This will greatly help the pressure that many women experience while using dating apps and sites.

3. Be Honest and Direct

When discussing boundaries, be honest and direct about your expectations. Clearly communicate what you are comfortable with and what is off-limits. Don't feel shy or scared to lose matches because you have them. Open communication builds trust and ensures mutual understanding.

4. Consent Is Ongoing

Consent is not a one-time agreement in dating, it is an ongoing process. You have to regularly update your matches or partner about your comfort levels and they should be receptive to any changes in your boundaries. Likewise, you must also check in with them. This ongoing communication is crucial for a healthy and respectful relationship no matter which phase your relationship is in.

5. The Power of Positive Language

If you fear communicating your boundaries because you don't want to lose matches, try using positive language. This will help you to convey your needs without sounding accusatory or sending matches into defense mode. For example, say "I prefer" or "I'm comfortable with" instead of focusing on what you don't want. Your words can make a huge difference in this case, so it is best to keep it positive!

6.   Set and Respect Time Boundaries

This is a big one that everyone misses and misunderstands. You need to set and respect each other's time boundaries. This will prevent bombarding someone with messages or expecting immediate responses. Online dating blurs this boundary in a way that makes it hard to understand what's going on. Should you message? Should you wait? Have they met someone else and are chatting to them instead? Does that sound familiar? Setting realistic expectations regarding response times helps create a balanced and respectful communication dynamic that won't have you holding onto your phone all day.

The Importance of Mutual Consent in Online Relationships

Mutual consent ensures that both individuals are comfortable with the pace and nature of the relationship. This has the ability to foster trust and create a foundation for a positive and potentially long-lasting connection.

The benefits of having mutual consent are:

- It builds trust because it shows that both individuals are considerate of each other's feelings, needs, and boundaries.

- It reduces the risk of misunderstandings by encouraging open and honest communication.

- It acknowledges that individuals have the right to make decisions about their own bodies, emotions, and personal space.

- It contributes to a positive and enjoyable experience for both parties.

You must always remember that levels of consent are different for different people. What you think is okay may not be the same for others. This is why it is crucial to have these conversations at different points when making online connections. When individuals feel heard, respected, and understood, it enhances the overall quality of the connection, making the online dating experience more fulfilling.

Safety Checklist

Ensuring your safety both on-and offline is of the utmost importance. However, we also understand that it's easy to forget all the steps when you're caught up in the excitement of meeting new and interesting people. This is why this safety checklist will come in handy during the different phases of online dating. Use it as a reminder of what needs to be done or communicated and you can always come back to it when you need it.

When You Register on a Dating App

- Define your boundaries and your dating goals.

- Use a trustworthy site or app.

- Set up your profile without disclosing personal information like your address, the company you work for, and your contact details.

- Decide which communication channels you want to use to communicate with matches.

- Ensure the photos you have on your profile do not disclose your address.

While Chatting to Matches

- Assess their profile looking for red flags.

- Do a little online research if you're unsure of the details provided.

- Ensure that you communicate your boundaries and are aware of theirs'. This includes sending and receiving pictures.

- Have time boundaries that ensure that you have time to chat with each other.

- Over time, make sure you communicate your dating timeline. This will ensure that no one rushes you into a meeting or talks off-platform too soon.

- Don't be afraid to report someone if they harass you online.

When You Decide to Meet

- Ensure that you are comfortable to meet and do not feel rushed.

- Choose a public space, preferably during the day.

- Use your own transportation.

- Tell someone where you are going and who you are meeting.

- Keep your personal belongings with you at all times.

- Have an exit plan should things get uncomfortable. For example, ask a friend to call you to check in and have a code word or phrase to let them know you want to leave.

- Always trust your gut and if you feel the need to leave, then leave. You don't have to feel guilty for trusting your instincts.

This checklist will help you remember what will ensure your safety at each step. Don't let anyone make you feel as if you are being paranoid by ensuring your safety. It is better to find matches who respect and understand your boundaries than those who criticize or mock them. Think of it as a way to narrow your list!

Now that you know how to stay safe while dating online, it's time to dive into the aspects that arise once you develop a relationship with a match. In the next chapter, we will be taking a look at how to handle long-distance relationships which are somewhat common for those who date online.

Chapter 5:

Long-Distance

Relationships

Absence sharpens love, presence strengthens it. -Thomas Fuller

One of the biggest advantages of online dating is that you get to meet people you would never have met under normal circumstances. They could live in a different state, a different country, or even an entirely different continent! However, as much as this is an exciting concept, long-distance relationships come with their own set of challenges. Understanding how to navigate long-distance relationships is crucial if you are using dating apps and sites that have a global user base. In this chapter, we will go through the methods you can use to ensure that your long-distance relationship has the best possible shot at success.

How to Make a Long-Distance Relationship Work

Long-distance relationships are not a new concept. They have been happening for centuries but the modern world has made it easier to stay connected. Online dating aside, long-distance relationships have become increasingly prevalent due to career opportunities in different places and going away to study. As a result, people have been navigating both the challenges and joys of maintaining romantic connections across geographical distances. These relationships take commitment, understanding, respect, trust, and a willingness to make an effort to make things work. Without these components—from both parties—it cannot possibly work. Thus, long-distance relationships are a matter of teamwork. However, if you and your partner are committed to making it work, it truly can be a rewarding experience that culminates in a strong and stable relationship.

In fact, statistics show that long-distance relationships have a similar success rate as any other relationship and don't have higher breakup rates than traditional relationships (Castillo, 2023). In addition, a whopping 3.75 million people are in long-distance marriages in the United States, meaning that spouses live in different states, cities, or countries. These statistics demonstrate not only how common long-distance relationships are but also how successful they can be. So, what makes them work out? Let's take a closer look at what they entail.

Psychological Aspects of Long-Distance Relationships

Long-distance relationships bring unique psychological challenges that can either strengthen or strain the connection between partners. Being aware of what it takes can help you decide if you are ready to embark on a long-distance relationship and help you sustain it. Here's what you need to know.

Trust

Trust is the cornerstone of any successful relationship, and in long-distance relationships, it takes center stage. The absence of physical presence requires a higher level of trust in your partner's commitment and faithfulness. Distance often makes people question the actions of their partner or create doubt. In addition, building trust in a long-distance relationship is also a bit different because you will not spend as much time together as you would with someone you are dating in the same location as you. This is where communication becomes crucial.

Communication

Effective communication becomes the bridge that sustains trust in long-distance relationships. Regular, honest, and open communication helps bridge the emotional gap created by physical distance. You need to find ways to stay connected and speak openly when something is bothering you. It is only through open communication that both of you can discuss the details necessary to make the relationship work and prevent doubt from weakening it.

Emotional Intimacy

Long-distance relationships often require a greater focus on emotional intimacy. Without the ability to engage in regular physical interactions, partners need to nurture their emotional closeness. This can be done through meaningful conversations, sharing thoughts and feelings, and actively participating in each other's lives from a distance. This may seem somewhat awkward if you're not quite accustomed to sharing your emotions but it is necessary for any form of meaningful relationship. Therefore, you should learn different ways to build emotional intimacy with your partner to strengthen your bond.

Independence and Autonomy

This one is a lot to handle mentally. Long-distance relationships often mean that you are in a relationship, but are literally physically single wherever you are. Being physically apart from your partner encourages the development of individual independence and autonomy. While this can be a positive aspect, it may also lead to feelings of loneliness in some people. The best way to describe it is being attached but still feeling physically alone.

This is a challenge of balancing personal growth while still maintaining your connection with your partner. Once again, this is where communication and emotional intimacy become important. Over time, you will learn how to retain the independence and autonomy you have developed while still being considerate of your relationship. As with all relationships, people have aspects of life outside their partner and the relationship to maintain their sense of self. Long-distance relationships require the same balance of togetherness and independence even though the scales are tipped more towards independence due to physical distance. You have to recognize this skewness and actively work to achieve the balance that will help you feel stable in your relationship and less alone in your independence.

Time Zones

If partners are in different time zones, coordinating schedules becomes a significant challenge. The inconvenience of time zone differences may lead to missed calls, delayed responses, and a sense of disconnection. As we discussed earlier, respecting schedules and time zone differences is crucial to building trust and understanding in communication. Likewise, successfully managing time zone challenges in long-distance relationships requires flexibility and understanding. You must not let it be a barrier to your relationship and careful planning will help you avoid feeling like you keep missing your time with your partner.

In a nutshell, long-distance relationships require a mindset shift. The psychological aspects listed above show you that a long-distance relationship can be fulfilling, as long as there is understanding, trust, communication, and emotional intimacy. These are things that require practice and patience. If you and your partner can achieve this, you have the foundation of a healthy and strong partnership that cannot be shifted by doubt.

Tips for Making Long-Distance Relationships Work

Here are some useful tips that will help make your long-distance relationship stand the test of time and distance!

Check-In With Each Other Regularly

Let's be clear, regular check-ins do not mean a status update every hour! You should aim to establish a routine for regular check-ins. This could include daily texts, scheduled phone or video calls, or even virtual dates. This type of realistic and consistent communication helps maintain a sense of connection and ensures that both partners feel involved in each other's lives.

Make Use of Technology

Technology has allowed us to have far more communication than long-distance relationships in the past where the only communication would be via post or very expensive phone calls! This is why you must make full use of technology to bridge the physical gap. Video calls, instant messaging, and social media platforms provide a means to stay visually connected and share daily experiences. You can also indulge in virtual activities, such as watching movies together or playing online games, to create shared moments despite the distance.

Set Clear Goals

As a couple, you need to define your relationship and set clear goals for the future. Knowing that the separation is temporary and having a plan for eventually being together, in one place, can provide a sense of purpose and direction. This eases the emotional burden of being apart and gives both of you something to work toward.

Create Shared Experiences

Technology is great for communicating and spending time together, but you should also make time for creating shared experiences. This could involve reading the same book, watching a TV series together, or even cooking the same recipe simultaneously. Shared activities contribute to a sense of connection and shared identity. It's also a fun way to stay connected through shared interests.

Surprise Each Other

Keep the element of surprise alive by sending unexpected gifts or letters. Small, thoughtful gestures go a long way in expressing love and commitment. Sending and receiving a surprise package can bring excitement and joy to both partners. It's a way to show your partner that you're thinking of them and that you can still spoil them from far away.

Visits

Whenever possible, plan visits to spend time together in person. These visits provide an essential opportunity to create memories, strengthen the emotional bond, and remind yourselves of the tangible aspects of the relationship. You both need to work together to determine what is feasible. Some couples alternate visits every month or so while others choose to meet at a halfway point between their locations for a shared vacation. It all depends on what is the most convenient and affordable for the two of you.

Patience Is Key

It's no secret that long-distance relationships require patience. Challenges will arise, and there may be moments of frustration and loneliness. Practicing patience and understanding that these feelings are temporary can help navigate the emotional highs and lows of distance. Communicating with your partner about your feelings will also help put you at ease.

Making a long-distance relationship work requires intentional effort. Online dating has proven time and again that love has no geographical limits anymore. With the right mindset, effort, and communication by both parties, you can make your long-distance relationship work. The moment it feels as if one person is making more of an effort than the other, there will be trouble in any type of relationship. With this in mind, you both can move forward with clear intentions and goals.

Virtual Date Ideas That Spark Connection

While dates in long-distance relationships are not traditional, they can still be pretty fun! Just as the COVID-19 pandemic taught us how to get creative with social gatherings online while on lockdown, virtual dates can help build the bond between a couple. We've already mentioned watching a movie together and cooking the same meal, so here are some great ideas for virtual dates.

- Visit a virtual museum together.

- Take online classes together. These can be a creative, or skill-building class—whatever you and your partner are interested in, really.

- Spend a date together playing games that allow you to learn about each other. For example, use a scenario generator to come up with different scenarios and take turns answering what you would do in each case.

- Play a virtual board game together. You can even invite your friends for a double date!

- Combining a surprise with a virtual date can also be great. Over time, you will get to know your partner's routines well. Order their favorite takeout and do the same for you, allowing you to share a surprise meal together.

- You can also purchase online art or craft kits and work on them together. Each of you can get a turn to choose a kit, thereby trying out each other's favorites.

- Exercising together, either via video calls or a shared online class, can be a great way to stay fit together and challenge each other.

- If you guys like puzzles, it is possible to do a virtual puzzle together or race each other if you like to compete.

- Sports fans can watch a game together.

- You can have a happy hour at home and get your friends to join in. This is a great way to de-stress after a difficult day or week and you can have a drink safely, in your own space, and with people you enjoy spending time with.

Virtual dates can help you stay close to your partner even though there is distance between you. This is by no means an extensive list, but just some ideas to help steer you in the right direction. It is easy to feel as if you're stuck in a rut in your long-distance relationship if you limit your interactions to just phone and video calls. Virtual dates provide opportunities to do exciting and enjoyable activities together. You get to share experiences and learn about your partner just as you would if they were in the same city as you.

Mapping Your Love: Future Planning

If your long-distance relationship is going great and you have found ways to connect and bond with your partner despite the distance, you're in a pretty good spot as a couple. However, the endgame of any long-distance relationship is to be together, in the same place eventually. It can't be long-distance forever and this has to be clear right from the very start—but how do you start planning the specifics of your future relationship? When does it begin? Who makes the move? Will you move in together right away? Many questions need to be answered. This is why it is important to have a plan for your future as a couple. Let's go over how to approach this situation and what you need to plan with your partner.

Actionable Steps to Planning Your Future With Your Long-Distance Partner

1.   Define the Long-Term Goal

As mentioned earlier in the chapter, setting relationship goals is important for couples in a long-distance relationship. It gives you both a future plan to work toward. To begin this process, have an open and honest conversation about the long-term goal of the relationship. Discuss your individual aspirations, career plans, and personal timelines. Define the parameters of the long-distance phase and mutually agree on the desired outcome, whether it's moving in together, getting married, or achieving a specific milestone. This may seem like it is too much too soon, but it is necessary when committing to a long-distance relationship.

2. Establish a Timeline

Work together to establish a realistic timeline for the future. Consider factors such as career goals, education, and any other commitments that may impact the timeline. Having a shared understanding of when the long-distance phase will end provides both partners with a sense of direction and purpose.

3. Financial Planning

Long-distance relationships often involve additional costs related to travel and communication. Discuss financial aspects openly, and plan for how you will manage these expenses. Consider budgeting for visits, planning for relocation costs, and exploring financial strategies that align with your goals. Not everyone likes talking about finances but these are the type of conversations that couples in a serious relationship need to have as they will impact both of your futures and plans.

4. Explore Relocation Options

If the ultimate goal is to eventually close the distance, you need to explore the potential relocation options. As a couple, you have to discuss which location makes the most sense for both of you in terms of career opportunities, personal preferences, and quality of life. Consider compromise and flexibility to find a solution that works for both of you.

5. Shared Responsibilities

Discuss and plan for shared responsibilities in the future, such as living arrangements, financial management, and household duties. Having a clear understanding of each other's expectations and responsibilities fosters a sense of teamwork and unity.

6. Cultural and Lifestyle Considerations

If your relationship involves being from different cultural backgrounds or lifestyles, discuss how these factors will be integrated into your future plans. Understanding and respecting each other's cultural values and preferences is crucial for a harmonious future together.

7. Legal and Immigration Considerations

If your relationship involves international borders, be aware of the legal and immigration considerations. You need to research the requirements for relocation or potential visa processes well in advance to avoid last-minute complications.

This is not a one-time conversation either. Communication throughout the relationship, as it develops, is necessary. You have to be honest with your partner and let them know what is important to you. Remember that a relationship is about compromise, flexibility, and understanding. However, this has to come from both individuals. Only then will you both be on the same page for your future together.

Some Inspirational Stories

To end this chapter, I wanted to go through some stories of successful long-distance relationships that started via online dating. This is to demonstrate that it is indeed possible and to help alleviate any hesitancy that you may have about the situation.

- Dan and Sarah met while at university in the United Kingdom. Sarah was from the United States and they decided to continue their relationship when she moved back. They spent 8 months as a couple together and a year long-distance before Sarah moved back to the UK. However, there was still distance between them even with the move. After 5 years, they are still together even though Sarah is back in the United States. They visit each other every 3-4 months and plan holidays together abroad (Sarah, 2020).

- Rich and Aindrea met on an online art forum as teenagers. Rich was from England and Aindrea lived in the United States. Their relationship blossomed over the course of seven years before they met in person in 2010. They married in 2011 and are still happily living together in England (*Our Long Distance Love Story*, 2018).

- Yasmin and Abdulahi met online in 2019. They lived in North Carolina and North Dakota, respectively. Their courtship was brief and entailed Abdulahi traveling to North Carolina twice in their first year of dating, and getting engaged soon after (Sarah, 2020).

All three of these stories demonstrate that each relationship has its own timeline and outcomes. Even though all three are successful relationships, they all entail different levels of togetherness, with Dan and Sarah still dating long-distance. Each couple will have their own version of their relationship and what feels right to them. Don't be afraid of dating long-distance as long as you and your partner have the trust, commitment, and understanding to make it work. In the next chapter, we'll be closing the distance and discussing how to maintain your relationship over time.

Chapter 6:

Maintaining Healthy

Relationships

Relationships are hard. It doesn't matter if they start online or not, they require understanding, maturity, trust, and open communication. Developing and maintaining a healthy relationship requires regular work, but having the right foundation and the right mindset toward it can make a significant impact. Furthermore, when it comes to online dating specifically, there are special considerations in terms of communication, trust issues, and arguments due to the nature of online communication. It's new territory for most of us to navigate but not impossible. There are several couples who have met online and have been able to maintain healthy long-lasting relationships and marriages. This means that you can, too, if you find the right partner and have the right approach to your relationship. In this chapter, we will discuss how you can maintain a healthy relationship both on and offline.

How to Chat: Communicating Online and Offline

We have already been through the art of effective communication online. However, the aim of this section is to highlight how to communicate both online and offline to maintain a healthy relationship. Communication is one of the major foundation blocks of relationships. It needs to be open, honest, and frequent—not only during arguments but consistently. Digital communication has opened up new avenues for connecting with others, bringing both opportunities and challenges to interpersonal relationships. This is why it is crucial to understand the differences between online and offline interactions. You need to understand when to use which and how to best use it while avoiding miscommunication.

Understanding the Dynamics: Digital vs. In-Person Communication

The first step in mastering the art of communication is recognizing the differences between digital and in-person interactions. While in-person communication allows for the exchange of non-verbal cues, such as facial expressions and body language, digital communication relies heavily on written words and emojis. The absence of these non-verbal cues can sometimes lead to misunderstandings and misinterpretations, making it important to approach digital communication with mindfulness and intention. We all know how a harmless word like "fine" can be interpreted wrongly if you don't know the tone behind it!

Best Practices for Digital Communication

When it comes to digital communication, you need to remember these best practices at all times.

Always Choose the Right Platform

With so many messaging apps and social media platforms available, it's essential to choose the right one for a particular conversation. Some platforms are better suited for casual banter, while others may be more appropriate for serious discussions. Don't have serious conversations over text when you know a call or video call would be better. Likewise, don't use video calls all day when a simple text will suffice, especially when your partner is at work.

Pay Attention to Your Tone

Unlike in face-to-face conversations where tone is conveyed through voice modulation and facial expressions, digital communication depends on the written word. Be mindful of the tone you use in texts and emails, as it can significantly impact how your message is received. Avoid using all caps, which may be interpreted as shouting, and consider using emojis to convey emotions.

Timing Matters

Understand that people have different schedules and priorities. Be respectful of their time by choosing appropriate times for sending messages. Avoid bombarding someone with messages and be patient if they don't respond immediately. Always remember that digital communication is not really the right platform for anything urgent. Thus, you can't get angry at someone for not responding immediately!

Be Clear and Concise

This is an important one. In the digital realm, attention spans are often shorter, and information overload is common. Keep your messages clear, concise, and to the point. It can be quite difficult to read a chunk of text without missing anything. If a more extended discussion is necessary, consider switching to a more suitable platform, such as a video call or an in-person meeting. This avoids misunderstandings and ensures that nothing is missed.

Embrace Video Calls

Video calls can be extremely beneficial when there is distance between partners. When a deeper level of communication is required, consider transitioning to video calls. Video calls allow for a more authentic connection by bridging the gap between digital and in-person communication. They enable you to see facial expressions, which adds a layer of emotional understanding that is often missing in text-based conversations.

These are the important aspects of digital communication that you need to keep in mind. We have been through the misuse of emojis already, but it is worth repeating that you should never overuse them, especially when having serious conversations. It is one of the easiest ways to be misunderstood online. You must also work toward not misinterpreting the tone of a message in the absence of vocal cues. If you're not sure, ask for clarification. There's no harm in making sure you understand the message correctly.

Best Practices for In-Person Communication

Talking to someone face-to-face can be difficult if you're shy, socially anxious, or if you don't have great communication skills. That's not something you should be ashamed of either because the digital age is partially to blame for that. When we get so used to communicating online, we forget what it's like to talk to someone in person. However, it remains an integral part of developing and maintaining a healthy relationship with your partner. Here are some tips for what you should aim for with in-person communication.

Active Listening

In any form of communication, active listening is a fundamental skill. When engaged in face-to-face conversations, make a conscious effort to focus on your partner, avoid distractions, and show genuine interest through non-verbal cues like nodding and maintaining eye contact. You'd be surprised at what a big difference this makes!

Emotional Intelligence

In-person communication allows for a delicate exchange of emotions between people. Practicing empathy by trying to understand your partner's perspective, and making use of emotional intelligence to navigate sensitive topics with care and consideration is crucial. By implementing this in your interactions with your partner, you are able to deeply connect and strengthen the bond you share. It brings a deeper understanding between both of you and allows you to navigate difficult situations easier.

Choose the Right Environment

This is an important one that most people seem to forget. The setting in which a conversation takes place can significantly impact its outcome. You need to choose environments conducive to open communication, free from distractions, and that will result in a comfortable conversation. We've all seen couples have arguments in public spaces or have heard of an awkward break-up in a quiet restaurant. You need to be mindful not only of your privacy but also of your ability to speak freely. The subject of the conversation must be taken into consideration when choosing where the discussion should take place.

Mind Your Words

In all interactions, words carry weight, but in in-person communication, their impact can be immediate. Choose your words carefully, be mindful of your partner's sensitivities, and avoid inflammatory language that may escalate tensions. There's no need to be harsh in any way, no matter the type of conversation you are having. Using hurtful words in this manner is not a sign of a healthy relationship because no one should want to hurt their partner, even when angry.

These are the most crucial elements of in-person communication. You have to be able to navigate digital and in-person communication when in a relationship. However, knowing in which context to use them is vital. You and your partner will find your rhythm of communication over time but you must never forget the above elements even when you find your comfort zone. This is important for maintaining a healthy relationship.

Maintaining Open Lines of Communication: Texting, Video Calls, and In-Person Talks

To maintain healthy relationships, it's essential to adapt communication strategies to the context and the nature of the relationship. Each mode of communication—texting, video calls, and in-person talks—has its own strengths and limitations. Let's take a quick look at them.

Texting

Texting allows you to be concise. You can send a message easily, it's less formal, and the use of emojis can be a great way to be playful with your partner. However, texts can also be misunderstood because of the lack of tone and the absence of body language. You also have to be mindful because some people find texts distracting and it may interrupt their work day or in extreme cases, their overall productivity.

Video Calls

These are great for in-depth conversations when there is distance between partners. You are able to see your partner as you speak, read their body language, and hear their tone as they speak. However, there are certain things you have to be aware of as well. If you choose to video call your partner, ensure that you choose a quiet, safe, and well-lit location and try to minimize distractions in your environment. This will allow you to focus on the conversation and maintain eye contact with your partner without having to worry about what's going on around you.

Face-to-Face Communication

The specifics of in-person communication are similar to video calls but having your partner physically in front of you provides a more personal environment. You are able to notice non-verbal cues and touch your partner as you speak. These are important aspects that can contribute greatly to a conversation. However, you still must aim to actively listen to your partner and not try to dominate the conversation. Somehow it becomes easier to interrupt someone while they are talking when you are in person. It is important to be mindful of this and try to stay present, allowing your partner to speak.

Tips on Navigating Challenges in Digital Communication

Misunderstandings are probably the biggest challenge of digital communication. It's easy to do when you can't hear the tone in which someone is speaking or know the situation they are replying. They could be in a rush and type out a quick text but you may find that it sounds cold or distant or they could miss your calls because they forgot their phone at home, but you may think they're avoiding you. These situations can be avoided if you have clear communication with your partner. The following tips can help you navigate sticky situations and help you build communication skills as a couple.

1. If you're unsure of something your partner says, ask follow-up questions for clarification. This is the easiest way to avoid misunderstandings. However, aim to watch your tone and ensure it is not accusatory.

2. Whenever you wish to discuss a problem with your partner use "I" statements. This is to ensure that they understand what you're trying to tell them and don't feel as if they're being blamed for something. For example, you can say, "I feel like you don't want to talk to me when you don't answer my calls," instead of, "You don't pick up the phone when I call."

3. Don't be hesitant to admit when you are wrong or misunderstand something. It is better to admit your mistake and discuss why it occurred

than to stay quiet about it. This will ensure clearer communication going forward.

4. Send voice notes instead of long messages. This can help to convey tone better than text, especially when they are long messages.

5. Get into the habit of re-reading a message before sending it. Sometimes we type out a text out of anger or hurt without really understanding the impact it may have. By building the habit of checking your message, you have time to pause and determine if your words are warranted or if you are reacting emotionally.

6. Do not have arguments over text! They never work out well. Schedule a phone call or meeting when you both have time. This will also give you time to regulate your emotions and ensure that you are not emotionally charged when the conversation occurs.

7. Be consistent in your communication. Do not start your relationship on a good foundation of communication and then let it dwindle over time. A healthy relationship requires consistent communication.

These tips are what you need to remember when it comes to communicating with your partner on different platforms. Know which platform is best for different types of discussions and don't take the easy way out just because it's more convenient. You don't want convenience, you need understanding and trust in your relationship!

Settling Arguments in the Screen Age

Conflicts are an inevitable part of any relationship. However, in the age of digital communication, it's essential to adapt traditional conflict resolution techniques so that they are equally as effective. We also have to approach digital conflicts with patience, empathy, and a willingness to understand different perspectives. We have gone through some of these techniques when we discussed best practices for communication, but they are worth mentioning again for their specific uses when dealing with conflicts.

1. Pause and Reflect

When faced with a conflict in digital communication, resist the urge to respond immediately. Take a moment to pause and reflect on the situation. This prevents impulsive reactions and allows for a more thoughtful and measured response.

2. Use Clear and Respectful Language

In written communication, clarity is important. Clearly express your thoughts and feelings without ambiguity or passive-aggressive language. You need to ensure that your message is respectful and avoids unnecessary escalation.

3. Avoid Assumptions

Ask open-ended questions to gain a better understanding of the other person's perspective. Avoid making assumptions, and actively listen to their concerns.

4. Establish Ground Rules

In ongoing relationships, consider establishing ground rules for resolving conflicts online. This might include agreeing on a designated time for addressing issues, avoiding public arguments on social media, and committing to maintaining a respectful tone in digital exchanges.

5. Don't Fight to Win

An argument is not supposed to be something that either partner wins. That would mean that someone loses, and that is not the aim of conflict resolution. You need to work together as a couple to solve the problem, gain a better understanding of each other, and understand why the problem arose in the first place. This will put you in a better position than before and stronger as a couple as you move forward.

6. Take Responsibility

If your words are harsh or cause a misunderstanding, take responsibility and apologize. Explain to your partner what led you to send the message and that the intent was not to upset them. You must focus on resolving the misunderstanding and learning to communicate better.

7. Don't Let Small Issues Accumulate

If there are little things that your partner does that do not sit right with you, don't push them aside out of fear of losing them. Those little things, whether it be a communication thing, something that they do that hurts your feelings, or something that causes doubt; can accumulate until they become unbearable. At this point, things may escalate quickly, leaving your partner confused as to why you are so angry or emotional. Discuss things as they arise so that you both get a better understanding of each other. Furthermore, it's generally easier to fix it when the issue is something small than when it becomes something much larger.

You need to grow together as a couple when it comes to conflict resolution. Both of you must learn to identify triggers and patterns that cause problems in your relationship and endeavor to learn from them. This will prevent the same arguments from arising and improve the way you communicate overall. A healthy relationship needs this, and it takes conscious effort. Be patient with each other and be willing to put in the work for a long-lasting relationship.

Social Media and Jealousy: How to Trust in a Digital Age

Social media has opened new avenues for communication and connection but has also brought about unique challenges for couples regarding trust and jealousy. This has to be addressed as social media enables couples to maintain a sense of connection, especially in long-distance relationships, making it an internal part of the relationship. However, the curated nature of social media, whereby we only see the positive aspects that people are comfortable sharing leads to comparison, feelings of inadequacy, and jealousy. This can even happen between partners as they perceive the other's experiences to be "better" than their own.

The other issue with social media is that it may blur lines in a relationship if boundaries have not been communicated. This may result in blurring the boundaries between public and private aspects of a relationship. In turn, it can create discomfort or conflict if one partner feels exposed or invaded. It is, therefore, necessary to have clear communication with your partner regarding social media usage as a couple. In this way, you will build a secure relationship based on the trust you have in each other.

How to Build Trust Online

Here are some practical steps to follow as a couple:

- **Set boundaries together**: First and foremost, establish boundaries regarding online interactions with others. This may include guidelines on connecting with ex-partners, responding to comments, or sharing personal details. Setting clear boundaries helps prevent potential sources of conflict.

- **Social media values**: This ties in with your boundaries but is also important to clarify with your partner. Discuss your values and expectations regarding social media use in your relationship. Establish common ground on issues such as privacy, posting about the relationship, and interacting with others online.

- **Communication**: This might seem repetitive but it really is that important. You need open and honest communication about your social media habits, including how frequently you use these platforms and what you share. Transparency builds trust and reduces the likelihood of misunderstandings.

- **Don't forget digital affection**: Demonstrate your commitment through digital gestures of affection, such as liking or commenting on your partner's posts. Including each other in your online presence fosters a sense of inclusion and reinforces the strength of your relationship.

These tips will help your relationship thrive despite the challenges of social media. Having a clear understanding between the two of you ensures that you have an unshakable foundation. However, despite your efforts, there might be other people who introduce jealousy into the equation, and that is also something you will both need to deal with.

Managing Jealousy: Strategies for a Healthy Digital Relationship

As much as some people think it's cute or "hot" if their partner gets jealous, jealousy is usually an unwelcome guest in any relationship. Unfortunately, social media has the potential to amplify its presence. Managing jealousy requires a combination of efforts. Let's take a look at what you can do, as a couple, to manage jealousy.

- **Reflect on the triggers**: Take time to reflect on the specific triggers that evoke feelings of jealousy. Is it certain types of interactions, specific posts, or patterns of behavior? If you know what your triggers are you can start addressing and managing jealousy.

- **Communicate feelings openly**: When feelings of jealousy arise, communicate openly with your partner. Share your emotions without blaming and express your concerns. A supportive partner will listen and work with you to find solutions.

- **Participate in trust-building practices**: This may include sharing passwords, discussing social plans, or making joint decisions about privacy settings. These practices can reinforce trust in your relationship.

As much as the above steps are important, you should also work on building individual confidence and self-esteem. A secure sense of self makes you less prone to episodes of jealousy. It also allows partners to celebrate each other's successes rather than viewing them as threats to their relationship.

Recognizing Red Flags on Social Media: Trust Issues to Watch For

While healthy relationships thrive on trust, certain behaviors on social media may signal underlying trust issues. It's important to be aware of potential red flags and address them proactively. Here's what you should look out for both in your partner and yourself.

1. **Excessive monitoring**: Constantly monitoring your partner's online activities, including checking their likes, comments, and followers, may indicate a lack of trust. Healthy relationships are built on mutual respect and privacy.

2. **Secretive behavior**: Hiding online interactions, concealing certain posts, or maintaining secret social media accounts raises concerns about transparency. Openness is vital in cultivating trust within a relationship.

3. **Frequent accusations**: Persistent and baseless accusations of infidelity or mistrust based on social media activities can indicate deeper insecurities. Healthy relationships require a foundation of trust and communication rather than constant suspicion.

4. **Control or isolation of social media**: Intentionally isolating a partner from online networks or discouraging social media use may be a sign of controlling behavior. Trust is built on mutual respect.

5. **Online and offline personas**: A big difference between your partner's online and offline behavior may raise concerns. If your partner presents a drastically different persona online, it's essential to explore the reasons behind this inconsistency.

These red flags should not be ignored. Instead, they should be approached with sensitivity and addressed through honest conversations. This will help you strengthen your relationships or highlight the cracks in them. Ultimately, it is through communication, whether digital or in person, that you will be able to find a way forward. If you cannot, it may be time to realize that this is not the healthy relationship that you desire. This brings us to the next chapter, where we will be discussing how to navigate breakups and have the courage to start again.

Chapter 7:

Breakups and Moving On

Going through a breakup, from the decline of the relationship to the eventual fallout, is incredibly draining. The range of emotions you experience is no different than the stages of grief and that's no surprise given that you are grieving a loss. Digital breakups are no different. Even those online matches at the start can leave you feeling broken when they don't work out because of the loss of the idea of being in a relationship. Online dating is a bit of an emotional rollercoaster. Not everyone will find the love of their life in the first week, let alone the first year of using a dating app.

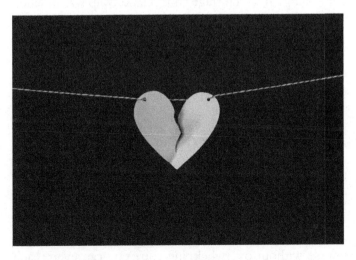

The time you spend on the app will lead to a number of "almosts" that end in heartbreak, either for one or both parties. However, this doesn't mean you should give up on trying to find your person. In this chapter, we will cover how to cope with online breakups and get back into the dating game afterward. Knowing how to do this is integral to your overall online dating experience.

Dealing with Digital Goodbyes: Coping With Online Breakups

When relationships occur primarily online, the emotional toll of parting ways can be uniquely intense. All the insecurities, doubts, and questions hit you all at once, and in many cases, there is no closure. Furthermore, depending on which stage your relationship was in when it ended, there are also digital reminders in the form of photos, text messages, and emails. To transition from being connected on multiple platforms to nothingness can also take its toll. Here are some practical steps that can help you with this process.

Managing the Emotional Toll

The absence of physical proximity does not diminish the depth of connection or the pain of separation. You need to allow yourself to grieve and process your emotions. Acknowledge that they are valid and let them run their course without overwhelming you. You can even reach out to friends or a trusted family member to share your feelings. The support of others can provide perspective, comfort, and a sense of connection to others.

During this time, you might also want to establish clear boundaries with your ex-partner to create space for healing. This may include limiting contact, both online and offline, to allow you both to move on. If the emotional toll becomes overwhelming over time, or you find it negatively affecting your daily life for an extended period, you should consider seeing a therapist. They will help you process your emotions and provide valuable tools for coping with grief, loss, and emotional distress.

What to Do With Old Texts and Pictures

We've all been there after a breakup, trying to figure out what to do with all the digital memories on our phones. If you're not ready to delete everything, organize and archive digital mementos in a separate folder. This allows you to preserve memories while creating the mental and emotional space for healing. In addition, you can come back to them when you are ready and be able to sort through them in a rational manner. Often, people delete photos and miss them later, not because of their ex, but because of the memories associated with them.

A digital detox is also another option to create space for healing. This temporary break prevents you from scrolling through old conversations and photos, reliving the past, and grieving the relationship. You can go back to them when you are ready to sort through them knowing that you won't make impulsive decisions regarding them and your past.

Adjust Privacy Settings

After a breakup, reviewing and adjusting your privacy settings on social media platforms is necessary. Depending on the nature of the breakup you may choose to unfriend or unfollow your ex, or you can consider limiting the visibility of your posts to control what your ex-partner can see. To some, unfollowing or unfriending an ex may seem like a harsh action, but it makes it easier to avoid emotional triggers for both of you. Another option is to make use of features such as mute or hide to minimize exposure to your ex-partner's content without the need for complete unfriending. This approach allows for a more gradual disengagement but still gives you space to heal.

Focus On Personal Growth

It is always a good idea to take some time after a breakup and focus on yourself. This is the time to self-reflect, acknowledge the lessons of your failed relationship, and focus on personal growth. Avoid comparing your post-breakup life to your ex-partner's online presence. Everyone navigates the healing process differently, and social media often portrays a curated version of reality.

You can shift from online interactions to offline activities that contribute to your overall well-being. Moving away from the digital realm can be healthy in situations where the online breakup is quite difficult or when time away from your ex is needed. If you focus on your personal growth, you can get back into the dating game stronger than before with a firm understanding of what is needed in a healthy relationship.

One common thread runs through these steps—taking a step away from the online world is necessary to give yourself the space needed to recover from a breakup. It's not about disappearing or completely deleting your online presence but rather using the time away to think about how to proceed. You will learn more about yourself, your mistakes, your reactions, and your emotions during this time. It's quite the process, but it will put you in a much better position moving forward.

The Self-Love Checklist: Caring for Yourself After a Breakup

Self-care after a breakup is crucial. Although most of us battle with the concept of self-care overall, it is not an indulgent or egotistical process. You have to take care of yourself in order to be the best possible version of yourself in everything that you do. This is not about putting on a brave face or pretending to be something that you are not. Instead, it is about genuinely taking care of yourself and rediscovering your sense of self outside your previous relationship. This process may look different for different people, but we have put together a list of self-care tips specifically curated for online breakups. Some of them were mentioned in the previous section where we discussed how to manage a digital breakup so we will not go into too much detail.

1. Gradually reduce your online interactions, especially those related to your ex-partner.

2. Reach out to friends, family, or a support network to share your feelings and experiences.

3. Set digital limits by establishing clear boundaries with your ex-partner to avoid unnecessary online interactions.

4. Spend quality time with friends and family, or engage in activities that bring joy and fulfillment.

5. Use a journal as a therapeutic outlet for processing emotions, gaining clarity, and tracking personal growth.

6. Seek the guidance of a therapist or counselor to obtain a structured space for processing emotions, gaining insights, and developing coping strategies.

7. Practice mindfulness and meditation to help promote emotional regulation, reduce stress, and cultivate a present-moment awareness.

8. Make time to exercise. Engaging in physical activity releases endorphins, improves mood, and contributes to overall well-being.

9. Channeling emotions into creative outlets, such as art, writing, or music, allows for self-expression and acts as an emotional outlet.

10. Embrace a growth mindset that views challenges as opportunities for learning and personal development. This will allow you to look at your past relationship as a lesson.

11. Reflect on your core values, aspirations, and long-term goals. Reconnect with the essence of who you are independent of the relationship.

12. Engage in new experiences that offer adventure, exploration, and an opportunity to embrace curiosity. It's not about being risky or thrill-seeking but more of a way to learn more about yourself as you step out of your comfort zone.

These self-care tips will help you focus your energy on letting go of the past and embracing the person it made you. There is time to acknowledge your heartbreak and emotions, process them, and start reassessing your personal goals. However, you must remember that healing is a gradual process, and different for everyone. Don't compare yourself to others or even your ex. It's okay to seek support from friends, family, or a therapist. This will only help you further when set clear intentions for your future, including your future dating endeavors.

Stepping Back Into the Dating Game

Breakups, whether they occur in person or online, mark the end of one chapter and the beginning of another. It's an important reminder that life—and love—goes on. After the emotional process of healing and self-discovery, the prospect of reentering the dating game can be both exciting and daunting. However, before you begin, you must ensure that you have let go of the emotional baggage of your previous relationship. This would entail letting go of past mistakes after learning from them and acknowledging the relationship was not meant to be.

You have to reenter the dating scene with a positive mindset and not with one that questions your every action. The journey of self-discovery after a breakup should have provided you with closure and understanding of the end of your previous relationship. Therefore, you have learned from it and know that you will not make the same mistakes again, or be able to better recognize red flags that need to be addressed. Having this mindset allows you to move forth with confidence and a positive outlook toward dating again instead of being scared and limiting your dating experiences.

A Step-by-Step Guide to Reentering the Online Dating Scene

Here's what you need to do when you're ready to start dating again.

Redefine Your Dating Goals

Before you jump back into online dating, it is essential to redefine your relationship goals. This requires self-reflection and the knowledge you have gained from your previous relationships. Consider what you seek in a partner, the type of relationship you envision, and the values that are important to you. These would have changed slightly after a breakup and your online dating experience thus far. Identify aspects that were fulfilling and those that contributed to challenges. You can then use this to redefine your dating goals.

Update Your Online Profile

Once your dating goals are set, it's then time to update your online dating profile. Update your photos, ensuring that they are recent, write a genuine bio, and highlight your interests and values. You want to infuse your profile with a positive tone. Focus on your passions, hobbies, and the qualities you appreciate in a potential partner. Positivity is attractive and invites like-minded individuals.

Choose a Dating Platform

We already know that different platforms cater to various demographics and relationship types. Your previous experiences will also be able to help you decide which platform best suits your needs. However, don't be afraid to try new platforms as well. Things may have changed since your profile was last active and you need to do a bit of research to choose the right platform again.

Take Your Time

This is important. Don't be in a hurry to get back into a relationship. You should allow relationships to unfold naturally. Take your time and don't start a relationship just for the sake of it. You don't want to be the person who uses someone else as their rebound nor do you want to get into a meaningless relationship just because you want to prove a point to your ex. Comparing yourself to others is the quickest way to be unhappy. Being in an empty relationship just to post photos will leave you feeling miserable and possibly lonelier than being single. Thus, take your time and be intentional about who you interact with. If you're dating just to jump back on the wagon and don't want anything serious, be clear about that with your matches, and don't lead them on.

Have Conversation Starters

You should consider creating conversation starters that are personalized and genuine. Frame questions in a way that encourages open-ended responses. This promotes meaningful conversations and allows you to get to know the person on a deeper level. Let your personality shine through your messages, as this is what will help you connect with people.

Have a Positive Mindset

As you reenter the dating world, approach it with an open mind. Be willing to meet individuals with diverse backgrounds, interests, and perspectives. Embrace the potential for unexpected connections and don't ruminate on the past. View each date as a learning opportunity. Regardless of the outcome, each interaction contributes to your understanding of yourself and your preferences. An understanding that not every connection will lead to a long-term relationship, and that's okay. Rejection is a natural part of the dating process and an opportunity for growth.

Don't Talk About Your Ex

You should avoid comparing new connections to past relationships. Each person is unique, and making comparisons may hinder your ability to appreciate someone for who they are. Mature relationships may turn to previous relationships, but there is no need to talk about your ex. Discussing what you have learned from what went wrong is a better conversation that demonstrates personal growth. If you talk about your ex-partner, your current match may think that you are not over your breakup or that you still have feelings for someone else. This hinders the entire dating process.

Stepping back into the dating game after an online breakup is a journey of self-discovery, renewal, and the potential for new connections. By approaching this phase with a positive mindset and embracing the lessons learned from past experiences, you can have a great online dating experience again. Don't be in a hurry, though. Take things at a pace you are comfortable with and always keep communication open and honest. This will ensure that your intentions are always known whether you're dating casually or looking for a serious relationship.

Breakups cannot be avoided in the dating game, it's actually an integral part of it. Without experiencing heartbreak and rejection, we cannot build emotional resilience. Furthermore, it is through breakups that we learn about what we don't want in a relationship and learn to better recognize the red flags that signal relationship issues. This will only help your future relationships.

Chapter 8:

Love in the Digital Age

Dating, falling in love, and finding your happily ever after is not something you can predict. Every relationship is different and the outcome is not known, which is why dating is considered a risk. You have to be willing to put your heart on the line in order to figure out whether your happily ever after is within reach. Online dating has made it easier to meet new people at a time when there is no time for anything. However, it has also made people choose potential partners differently. Online dating makes it possible to actively search for love. You're stating your desired traits and listing yours, making the matching progress much more intentional. Even though not every match is a success, it is possibly still better than traditional dating where you start off knowing very little, if anything at all, about someone.

This is why love in the digital age is easier to come across but sustaining this love and transforming it into a healthy, long-lasting relationship may be a bit more difficult due to the unique challenges involved. However, that does not mean it's impossible. Several couples have found love, stable relationships, and their life partners online. They each had to overcome their own unique challenges to maintain their relationship but they were all committed to doing so. In this chapter, we will be going through some of these remarkable success stories to give you some inspiration to embark on your own journey to love.

Real-Life Romances: Success Stories and Testimonials

Everyone loves a good love story, the "meet-cute" that we are familiar with because of movies and social media. These moments also occur online and not just in advertisements for dating apps and sites. Let's take a look at some of the online success stories that will give you the motivation to get back into the dating game and some important lessons!

For the Love of Books

Mariana first noticed Rafael on Tinder because of a picture of his extensive library. Also having a love of books, she swiped right and they started chatting. Rafael only waited a few days before asking her out for a coffee date, but Mariana turned him down because she wasn't into coffee. However, she didn't explain this to him and Rafael though she just didn't want to go out with him. Mariana eventually asked Rafael out for a beer and they have been dating ever since despite the initial mix-up (Purewal, 2016).

Lessons:

- They bonded over a shared interest.

- Despite their connection and initial chatting, the lack of effective communication made Rafael believe that Mariana was not into him.

Don't be Afraid to Make the First Move

Rozie was on a Jewish dating site and was waiting for her membership to expire. She was not enjoying the search process and had no luck with partners. Her one last attempt was to send Todd an email after seeing his profile picture and finding him attractive. Todd was reluctant to reply to the email because Rozie's profile was pretty scant—she didn't even have a profile photo! However, Todd decided he'd reply to the email and ask for a picture. He obviously liked what he saw because they started exchanging emails after.

A month later, they had their first date. It was supposed to be a quick, casual date but ended up lasting seven hours! It also seems like seven is their number because, after seven months of dating, Todd proposed to Rozie (Spira, 2014)!

Lessons:

- Choosing a dating site that is tailored to what you are looking for is pivotal.

- As much as online dating can be frustrating, don't give up! Your person may be the next match you make!

- A profile that is missing all the details raises suspicion and may count against you.

- A first date should happen when you are comfortable taking things offline. Every relationship has its own timeline.

Give Long-Distance a Shot

Christina's friend was actually scrolling through her dating app when she spotted Daniel, someone she had met while studying in another country. She persuaded Christina to chat with him online, so she liked his profile. The two started chatting and quickly set up their first date in San Francisco where they were both based. However, after dating for five months, Daniel had to go to Spain to complete his studies. The two decided to end their relationship, knowing that it would be too difficult to maintain with the massive time difference.

Little did the two expect that they would still keep in contact daily, despite the time difference. Christina ended up going to Spain for her birthday and the two spent time together, realizing that ending their relationship was a mistake. Therefore, they decided to try the long-distance thing and about a year later Christina moved to Spain to be with Daniel before the two moved back to the United States together (Edmonds & Johnson, 2023).

Lessons:

- Luck sometimes plays a factor in finding your match. If Christina's friend hadn't told Christina she'd met Daniel before, she may not have messaged him.

- Long distance is not as difficult as most people think it is. If both partners are committed to making it work, it will!

These are just a few of the stories that I came across online. What I liked about them, and why I found them inspirational, is that all three of them demonstrate how different an online relationship can be. There is no expected timeline or outcome. Each couple did things their own way and found their own path to love! You have to be willing to put yourself out there and keep trying until you get it right.

Authenticity in a Digital Space

We have discussed the importance of authenticity multiple times thus far. However, this section will aim to summarize what we have learned and what you need to always keep in mind when it comes to online dating. Authenticity is a guiding principle, shaping the quality and depth of connections in online dating. At its core, it refers to the genuine expression of one's true self, beliefs, and intentions.

In the context of online dating, authenticity manifests in various ways, such as:

- Your profile.

- The information you provide.

- The photos you post.

- Your interests.

- The conversations you have both on and offline.

If you do not exhibit authenticity in your online dating attempts, you will never have an authentic match or have it lead to an authentic relationship. pending to be someone you're not in hopes of gaining more interest will only set you up for disaster. You will have to continuously be someone you are not, and this is exhausting. Furthermore, you are misleading someone else by letting them believe that they have found an authentic match. This will only lead to empty relationships and messy breakups at some point.

Tips on Spotting Authenticity Online and in Conversations

Here's what you need to look out for:

- Genuine people usually have photos that match the information provided in their profile.

- When you meet them, you realize they look like their photos.

- They want to find out more about you and ask earnest questions.

- They don't avoid your questions.

- People who are on an online dating site looking for a relationship are not going to make odd requests such as asking for intimate photos, enquiring about your finances, or asking to move off the platform immediately.

- Perfection can also be a red flag. Sure, you might come across a few people who live an ideal life, but they genuinely are transparent about it. Photos are unfiltered, demonstrating real situations, and the information is credible.

- They won't avoid video calls.

- Genuine people will not try to get your physical address or exact location.

The online world provides many opportunities for people to hide behind untruths. Always trust your instincts when you're talking to people. If something doesn't sit right with you ask them about it or do a little online digging to figure out if what they're telling you is real or not.

Looking Ahead: What the Future Holds for Online Love

As technology continues to advance, online dating will continue to transform in order to enhance our experiences. What exactly will this look like? Well, we can't tell for sure what will work and what won't, but it sure does sound exciting! Let's take a look at how online dating is set to evolve and what this means for your dating life.

Emerging Trends in Online Dating and Social Media

1. The Use of Augmented Reality (AR)

Augmented Reality can provide users with real-time information about potential matches in their physical vicinity, creating a more dynamic and interactive dating environment. In addition, AR has the potential to make profiles more engaging, fostering a deeper understanding before the first conversation. AR can also be used for virtual date planning, allowing users to explore shared virtual spaces or activities before deciding to meet in person. This will help those who don't know how to do this on their own and keep all interactions on one platform.

2. Integration of Virtual Reality (VR) in Dating Experiences

Virtual Reality differs from augmented reality in that it will put users in a simulated environment as opposed to a live current feed. This opens up the possibility of users meeting and interacting in a digital space that mimics real-world settings, providing a unique and immersive dating experience. If this pans out well, VR will eliminate geographical barriers, allowing individuals to connect on a much larger global scale than it does already. VR could also be used to create scenarios that help individuals assess compatibility on a deeper level. From shared activities to virtual travel experiences, these simulations could provide valuable insights into relationship dynamics. Imagine how amazing it would be to find out what it is like to live with someone without having to move to a different country!

3. AI-Powered Matchmaking Algorithms

Artificial Intelligence is slowly integrating itself into various applications and online dating is no exception. It has the greatest potential to refine matchmaking algorithms. AI can analyze user data, preferences, and behaviors to offer highly personalized recommendations, increasing the likelihood of meaningful connections. It can predict compatibility based on a multitude of factors, from communication styles to long-term relationship goals. These predictive models aim to enhance the overall accuracy of matchmaking. In addition, as AI algorithms learn from user interactions and feedback, they adapt and improve over time. This continuous learning process refines the matchmaking experience, ensuring that recommendations align with ever-evolving user preferences.

4. Video-First Communication

The trend toward video-first communication is gaining momentum. Dating apps are incorporating video features that allow users to share short clips or engage in live video chats, providing a more authentic and immediate connection. While this may make some people uncomfortable, it is much harder to lie via video than it is via text. It enables users to gauge body language, expressions, and tone of voice, fostering a deeper level of connection compared to text-based communication. Video features would also be able to facilitate virtual dates on the platform, making it easier for users to develop connections.

5. Enhanced Security Measures

As security issues online continue to rise due to numerous threats, dating apps may decide to implement enhanced security measures. The future of dating may see increased emphasis on biometric verification to enhance security. This could involve facial recognition or fingerprint scanning to ensure that users are who they claim to be, mitigating risks associated with catfishing or deceptive practices. Dating platforms may even integrate more robust background check features, providing users with additional information about potential matches. This move towards enhanced security measures aims to create a safer and more transparent online dating environment.

6. Biometric Feedback in Dating Apps

This one could be pretty helpful for those who battle to "read" people online. Future dating apps may incorporate biometric feedback, such as emotion recognition technology. This could analyze facial expressions and physiological responses during video interactions, providing insights into the emotional dynamics of a conversation. It could also evaluate how individuals respond emotionally to each other, offering additional layers of insight into the potential success of a match.

These are all exciting possibilities that you have to look forward to in the future. Technology is constantly evolving and dating apps will always try to refine their processes to improve success rates and make things easier for their users. It is then up to you to ensure that you stay up-to-date with these changes so that your online dating experience reaches its full potential.

Adapting to Changing Trends: Tips for Maximizing Digital Love Opportunities

With anything these days, you have to keep up or be left behind. Online dating is no different. If you want to achieve positive results, you have to ensure that you keep learning and keep your profile updated to reflect this. As our final step, let's take a look at how you can adapt to changing online dating trends and stay on top of your dating game.

7. Stay Informed and Willing to Embrace Change

You have to stay informed about emerging trends in online dating and be open to exploring new features and technologies as they become available. Embrace a growth mindset as you continue to learn and grow over time. When you are open to change and being out of your comfort zone, you are able to embrace the new and exciting opportunities it brings.

If you're not sure how to approach these changes, just ask. There are online communities or discussion forums you can join where individuals share experiences and insights related to changing trends in digital love. By engaging in these discussions you can enjoy a sense of community and shared knowledge.

8. Practice Self-Awareness

You need to have regular check-ins with yourself. If things aren't working out the way you expect, you need to pause and self-reflect on your dating patterns and partner preferences. In doing so, you might be able to pinpoint areas you need to work on or where you need to adapt to a new trend that you may have missed on an updated dating app or site. This act allows you to be more self-aware in your actions online while also allowing you to embrace changes and achieve personal growth.

9. Always Keep It Real

No matter what update you are adapting to, don't be fake. As technology evolves, the core principle of authenticity remains timeless. Express your true self in your online presence, whether through text, images, or video. Authenticity forms the foundation of meaningful connections and will make a big difference in the people you attract.

10. Don't be Afraid to Embrace Technology

The future of online dating may bring novel approaches to connection and dating, and adaptability is key to navigating these changes. Don't be afraid to try out different platforms, different types of communication, and new profile structures. These changes are the things that will increase the size of your dating pool and increase your chances of finding a suitable match.

11. Prioritize Safety and Privacy

Lastly, no matter the changes that occur, don't forget to prioritize your safety and privacy online. Regularly review and update your security settings on dating platforms after platform updates and the introduction of new features. By doing this you ensure that you minimize risk while maximizing the use of new technologies. Once again, it's all about balance!

Looking into the future, online dating is filled with innovation, possibilities, and transformative technologies. The key to navigating this ever-evolving online world lies in adaptability, curiosity, and a commitment to authenticity. If you can achieve these three things, you have everything it takes to have a wonderful online dating journey in front of you!

Conclusion

The pursuit of love in the digital age is tricky if you don't know what you're doing. It's not about being technologically advanced or taking quality photos but instead, it comes from knowing how to showcase your authentic self and what you are looking for in a relationship. This is the lesson I learned in my own online dating journey and what led me to my spouse. You now have the tools required to pursue this for yourself. This book serves as a guide on your journey and will help you as you weave through the intricacies of crafting genuine profiles, fostering transparent communication, and nurturing connections that go beyond the surface. It is up to you to find balance in your path.

Authentic online dating and finding love in the digital world is not merely a quest for a romantic partner but a journey of self-discovery and renewal. It is only through self-reflection that you are able to identify what you are looking for in a partner. Even through difficult breakups and starting all over again, there is happiness to be found. You have to embrace these things as learning experiences that are crafting you and your dating life into a masterpiece of understanding, communication skills, and an open heart. It is only when you adopt this mindset that you can achieve personal growth and self-awareness, which are necessary for dating.

This book has given you all the tips, steps, and knowledge you need to get started with online dating. It's time to shake off the fear and doubt and embrace a new, empowered you. One that is ready to find love and happiness in the digital world. So, what are you waiting for? Go on, take that first step, update your online profiles, and put yourself out there! Your perfect match could be just a click away. I look forward to hearing all your online dating stories and would appreciate it if you let me know how this book helped you on your journey!

Glossary

- **Authenticity**: The ability to be true to one's self or personality.

- **Autonomy**: Freedom to make your own decisions, independent from others.

- **Bombarding**: To constantly or persistently act upon something, to overwhelm.

- **Compatibility**: The ability of something to exist in harmony with another.

- **Dynamics**: The pattern or trajectory of growth or change.

- **Emoji**: A group of symbols or small images that are used in digital communication to help convey the emotion of the writer or act as a response to a message.

- **Emotional Intelligence**: The ability of a person to recognize, understand, and regulate their emotions.

- **GIF**: An image or short video used in digital communication to highlight emotions and jokes.

- **Ghosted**: To stop all forms of communication with someone without any forewarning or explanation.

- **Hook-Up**: In the dating world, refers to meet-ups for casual sex.

- **Intentional**: Done with a specific purpose.

- **LGBTQ+**: Abbreviation for lesbian, gay, bisexual, transgender, queer and others.

- **Pseudonym**: A pen name or fictitious name taken on to conceal the real one.

- **Red Flag**: A warning sign or sign for alarm.

- **Situationship**: An undefined relationship where no titles are given.

- **Spatial**: Refers to something occupying space or a specific place.

- **Subscription**: An agreed-upon recurring payment in exchange for a service or use of something.

- **Temporal**: Time-related.

References

Alnuweiri, T. (2018, January 26). *Dating app tip: Send GIFs.* Well+Good. https://www.wellandgood.com/dating-apps-gifs-tips/

Anderson, M., & Vogels, E. A. (2020, March 6). *Young women often face sexual harassment online – including on dating sites and apps.* Pew Research Center. https://www.pewresearch.org/short-reads/2020/03/06/young-women-often-face-sexual-harassment-online-including-on-dating-sites-and-apps/

Andre, L. (2021, March 26). *141 Crucial Online Dating Statistics: 2023 Data analysis & market share.* Finances online. https://financesonline.com/online-dating-statistics/#

Baluch, A. (2023, July 19). *HER dating review.* Forbes Health. https://www.forbes.com/health/dating/her-dating-review/

Barnes, M. (2023, June 1). *51 Best virtual date night ideas in 2024 (that don't suck).* Science of People.

https://www.scienceofpeople.com/virtual-date-ideas/

Barnes, Z. (2016, January 9). *8 Ways to create an amazing online dating profile.* SELF. https://www.self.com/story/8-ways-to-create-an-amazing-online-dating-profile

Bird, M. (2023, April 22). *People say these are the red flags you should always look out for on dating apps.* BuzzFeed. https://www.buzzfeed.com/michelelbird/online-dating-red-flags

Calo, C. (2021, October 28). *eHarmony statistics 2023 & fun facts you didn't know.* Way Too Social. https://www.waytoosocial.com/eharmony-statistics/

Castillo, L. (2023, December 9). *Long distance relationships statistics [Fresh Research].* Gitnux.org. https://gitnux.org/long-distance-relationships-statistics/

Dark side of online dating: These 7 real-life stories will make you uninstall your dating app! (2018, July 6). The Times of India. https://timesofindia.indiatimes.com/life-style/relationships/dark-side-of-online-dating-these-7-real-life-stories-will-make-you-uninstall-your-dating-

app/photostory/64885324.cms?picid=6488537
8

Dixon, S. J. (2023, November 6). *Topic: Tinder.* Statista.
https://www.statista.com/topics/10082/tinder
/#topicOverview

Edmonds, L., & Johnson, J. (2023, February 14). *From a onesie bar crawl to crossing time zones, 7 couples who met on Tinder share how they fell in love.* Insider.
https://www.insider.com/tinder-couples-share-love-stories-dating-app-hits-10-years-2022-9#

Gilbert, N. (2021, March 30). *97 OkCupid statistics you must learn: 2023 Market share analysis & data.* Financesonline.com.
https://financesonline.com/okcupid-statistics/

Gould, W. R. (2022, November 14). *What Is ghosting?* Verywell Mind.
https://www.verywellmind.com/what-is-ghosting-5071864

Greene, J. (2023, March 28). *Are you in a "situationship"? Experts share 10 signs to look out for.* TODAY.com.
https://www.today.com/life/relationships/situationship-rcna53878#

Hadji-Vasilev, A. (2022, June 23). *25 Online dating statistics, facts & trends for 2022.* Cloudwards.

https://www.cloudwards.net/online-dating-statistics/#

Herrman, J. (2023, August 23). *Welcome to the age of AI-powered dating apps.* Intelligencer; Intelligencer. https://nymag.com/intelligencer/2023/08/welcome-to-the-age-of-ai-powered-dating-apps.html

Indah, K. (2023, November 10). *How many people use Hinge in 2024? (Users Statistics) - EarthWeb.* Earthweb. https://earthweb.com/hinge-users/

Kaur, D. (2021, March 16). *Going through a virtual heartbreak? These 3 tips will help you deal.* Healthshots. https://www.healthshots.com/mind/emotional-health/online-dating-101-how-to-deal-with-virtual-heartbreak/

Khalatian, I. (2023, March 17). *Matchmaking 2.0: How AI is revolutionizing online dating.* Forbes. https://www.forbes.com/sites/forbestechcouncil/2023/03/17/matchmaking-20-how-ai-is-revolutionizing-online-dating/?sh=13032ea345e8

Manik, A. (2022, September 28). *Wanna up your dating game? 6 amazing ways to start a meaningful conversation on dating apps.* IDiva. https://www.idiva.com/relationships-love/relationships/amazing-tips-to-start-a-meaningful-and-engaging-conversation-on-dating-apps/18042408

McClain, C., & Gelles-Watnick, R. (2023, February 2). *2. The experiences of U.S. online daters.* Pew Research Center. https://www.pewresearch.org/internet/2023/02/02/the-experiences-of-u-s-online-daters/

McKay, L. (2018, July 19). *16 fast ways to resolve long-distance relationship fights.* Lasting the Distance. https://lastingthedistance.com/long-distance-relationship-fighting-arguments/

Miller, A. M., Blumberg, P. O., & Mejia, N. (2021, October 5). *If your partner does these 9 things, you could be in a "situationship."* Women's Health. https://www.womenshealthmag.com/relationships/a27478820/situationship/

Mukherjee, S. (2019, November 20). *Real-life incidents that show the dangers of online dating that women face.* Bonobology.com. https://www.bonobology.com/dangers-online-dating-women-face/

Mutziger, A. L., John. (2023, May 31). *7 of the best ways to start a conversation on a dating app, according to relationship therapists.* Insider. https://www.insider.com/guides/health/sex-relationships/how-to-start-a-conversation-on-a-dating-app

Nelson, S. (2018, January 21). *10 ways to spot genuine people when you're online dating*. Hey Saturday. https://www.heysaturday.co/10-ways-date-genuine-people/

Orlando, A. (2020, June 19). *10 benefits of online dating*. Marriage Advice. https://www.marriage.com/advice/relationship/benefits-of-online-dating/

Our Long Distance Love Story. (2018, September 5). From Long Distance to Marriage. https://www.longdistancetomarriage.com/our-story/

Pace, R. (2019, October 15). *Open communication in a relationship: How to make it work*. Marriage.com. https://www.marriage.com/advice/communication/open-communication-in-marriage/

Pace, R. (2021, December 28). *15 Tips to recover from a long-distance relationship breakup*. Marriage.com . https://www.marriage.com/advice/relationship/long-distance-relationship-breakup/

Plumridge, N. (2020, April 13). *Communication: Online vs. face-to-face interactions*. Psychminds.

https://psychminds.com/communication-online-vs-face-to-face-interactions/

Prendergast, C. (2023, April 11). *"Situationships" And "ghosting": The mental health impacts Of undefined relationships.* Forbes Health. https://www.forbes.com/health/mind/modern-dating-mental-health/

Purewal, S. J. (2016, August 3). *Dating app success.* Muscle & Fitness. https://www.muscleandfitness.com/women/dating-advice/10-real-stories-people-who-met-dating-app/

Sarah. (2020, May 31). *9 inspiring long distance relationship stories.* Endless Distances. https://www.endlessdistances.com/9-inspiring-long-distance-relationship-stories/

Short, K. (2022, November 10). *14 inspiring online dating success stories.* Best Company. https://bestcompany.com/online-dating/blog/online-dating-success-stories

Spira, J. (2014, August 11). *My 3 favorite online dating success stories.* DatingAdvice.com. https://www.datingadvice.com/advice/my-3-favorite-online-dating-success-stories

Spira, J. (2019, December 17). *How to know if someone is genuine in online dating.* https://www.datingadvice.com/online-dating/how-to-know-if-someone-is-genuine-online-dating

Statistic Brain. (2018, August 23). *Online dating industry report.* Statistic Brain. https://www.statisticbrain.com/online-dating-statistics/

Staudinger, S. (2017, April 12). *Man steals woman's purse on first Tinder date.* CBS58. https://www.cbs58.com/news/man-steals-womans-purse-on-first-tinder-date

Stouffer, C. (2023, July 10). *Romance scams in 2023 + online dating statistics - Norton.* Us.norton.com. https://us.norton.com/blog/online-scams/romance-scams

Thompson, R. (2020, September 16). *How to set boundaries in the early stages of dating.* Mashable SEA. https://sea.mashable.com/go-jek/12494/how-to-set-boundaries-in-the-early-stages-of-dating

Utreja, K. (2023, May 5). *Bumble revenue and usage statistics 2023.* Helplama.com. https://helplama.com/bumble-revenue-usage-statistics/

Vogels, E. A. (2021, January 13). The state of online harassment. *Pew Research Center.* https://www.pewresearch.org/internet/2021/0 1/13/the-state-of-online-harassment/

Vogels, E. A., & McClain, C. (2023, February 2). *Key findings about online dating in the U.S.* Pew Research Center; Pew Research Center. https://www.pewresearch.org/short-reads/2023/02/02/key-findings-about-online-dating-in-the-u-s/

Weingus, L. (2022, February 8). *What to do after a breakup: Your self-care guide.* Silk + Sonder. https://www.silkandsonder.com/blogs/news/ what-to-do-after-a-breakup-your-self-care-guide

Wong, K. (2022, July 31). *Is Match.com still the best dating app for serious relationships?* Mindbodygreen. https://www.mindbodygreen.com/articles/mat ch-dating-app-review#

Image References

cottonbro studio. (2021a). *Person Using a Smartphone with Dating-Matching App on Screen* [Image]. *Pexels.* https://www.pexels.com/photo/person-using-a-smartphone-with-dating-matching-app-on-screen-6833571/

cottonbro studio. (2021b). *A Sad Woman Looking at her Cellphone While Sitting on a Bed.* [Image]. *Pexels.* https://www.pexels.com/photo/person-using-a-smartphone-with-dating-matching-app-on-screen-6833571/

Du Preez , P. (2016). *Laughing by the tracks* [Image]. *Unsplash.* https://unsplash.com/photos/photo-of-man-and-woman-laughing-during-daytime--8UEuVWA-Tk

Fauxels. (2019). *Woman Using Virtual Reality Goggles* [Image]. *Pexels.* https://www.pexels.com/photo/woman-using-virtual-reality-goggles-3183164/

Gambardella, J. (2020). *Woman Looking At A Man Sitting By The Table* [Image]. *Pexels.* https://www.pexels.com/photo/woman-looking-at-a-man-sitting-by-the-table-5083914/

Ivas, B. (2023). *Couple Sitting by Table on Restaurant Terrace.* [Image]. *Pexels.* https://www.pexels.com/photo/couple-sitting-by-table-on-restaurant-terrace-17746232/

Krukau, Y. (2020). *Photo of Woman Using Smartphone and Laptop* [Image]. *Pexels.*

https://www.pexels.com/photo/photo-of-woman-using-smartphone-and-laptop-4458393/

Milton, G. (2021). *Busy freelancer working on laptop at home* [Image]. *Pexels.* https://www.pexels.com/photo/busy-freelancer-working-on-laptop-at-home-7034430/

Miroshnichenko, T. (2020). *A Woman Holding on A Man's Arm in Walking* [Image]. *Pexels.* https://www.pexels.com/photo/a-woman-holding-on-a-man-s-arm-in-walking-5698206/

Nic. (2022). *A cell phone sitting next to a keyboard* [Image]. *Unsplash.* https://unsplash.com/photos/a-cell-phone-sitting-next-to-a-keyboard-Ln2v2Bgi8hU

Piacquadio, A. (2020). *Side View Photo of Smiling Woman in a Black and White Striped Top Sitting on a Bed While Using a Laptop* [Image]. *Pexels.* https://www.pexels.com/photo/side-view-photo-of-smiling-woman-in-a-black-and-white-striped-top-sitting-on-a-bed-while-using-a-laptop-3765035/

Podrez, A. (2021). *Man on a Video Call* [Image]. *Pexels.* https://www.pexels.com/photo/man-on-a-video-call-6585019/

RDNE Stock project. (2021). [*city man couple hands*] [Image]. *Pexels.* https://www.pexels.com/photo/city-man-couple-hands-6415617/

Shvets, A. (2020). *Photo of Women Embracing While Standing on Beach* [Image]. *Pexels.* https://www.pexels.com/photo/photo-of-women-embracing-while-standing-on-beach-3727541/

Sikkema, K. (2018). [broken heart hanging on wire] [Image]. In *Unsplash.* https://unsplash.com/photos/broken-heart-hanging-on-wire-E8H76nY1v6Q

Surface. (2021). [*person sitting on couch holding a surface device*] [Image]. *Unsplash.* https://unsplash.com/photos/person-sitting-on-couch-holding-a-surface-device-8HPLpr3hebU

Thian , M. (2018). [*woman sitting on couch while using laptop computer*] [Image]. *Unsplash.* https://unsplash.com/photos/woman-sitting-on-couch-while-using-laptop-computer-U7lWyAV-aM8

Thought Catalog. (2018). [*woman sitting on floor and leaning on couch using laptop*] [Image]. *Unsplash.* https://unsplash.com/photos/woman-sitting-on-floor-and-leaning-on-couch-using-laptop-Nv-vx3kUR2A

van Schoonderwalt, M. (2020). *Red Flags on Flagpoles* [Image]. *Pexels.* https://www.pexels.com/photo/red-flags-on-flagpoles-5504680/

Winkler, M. (2020). *Black ipad on brown wooden table* [Image]. *Unsplash.* https://unsplash.com/photos/black-ipad-on-brown-wooden-table-qBw6Gy5zpVM

Made in the USA
Las Vegas, NV
28 March 2025

20242246R00098